What's left of
NELSON

*A full-length portrait of Nelson
painted immediately after the Battle of the Nile.
National Maritime Museum*

LEO MARRIOTT

**DIAL
HOUSE**

First published 1995

ISBN 0 7110 2303 4

Published by Dial House
an imprint of Ian Allan Ltd,
Terminal House, Station
Approach, Shepperton,
Surrey TW17 8AS.
Printed by Ian Allan Printing
Ltd, Coombelands House,
Coombelands Lane,
Addlestone, Weybridge, Surrey
KT15 1HY.

Front cover:
Portrait of Nelson by Abbott.
National Maritime Museum
Nelson's Column. *S. Forty*
HMS *Victory. M. Stride*

CONTENTS

Acknowledgements

In the search for information and material for this book I have been assisted by the efforts of a remarkable cross-section of people, all of whom share an interest in the life and achievements of Nelson. I have been particularly struck at how proud people are to be associated in some small way with the man and I hope that they will find something of interest within the pages of this book. In particular I would like to thank the following, listed in no particular order, for their efforts on my behalf:

Alan Piggot, Secretary The Nelson Society; Chris Lewis, Curator of the Maritime Museum of East Anglia; Mr Curtiss, Curator Lloyd's Collection; Eric Waters, Curator Bucklers Hard Maritime Museum; Lt M. R. Honnoraty, RN, HMS *Trafalgar*; Colin White, MA, AMA, Head Curator, Royal Naval Museum; Hazel Garlick, Royal Naval Museum; Chris Grey, National Maritime Museum, Greenwich; Lt J. Haynes, Executive Officer, HMS *Victory*.

Bibliography

It had been my intention to provide a list of all the biographies and other books dealing with Nelson as an appendix to this book. Like many other ideas, this fell by the wayside as the sheer quantity of such publications became apparent and complete listing could probably fill a substantial part of this book alone. However, during the course of research I made use of a variety of publications, of which the following were the most significant. In each case I am pleased to record my thanks to the efforts and original work of the authors involved.

Bob Brister. *Nelson's Norfolk*. Bob Brister Publications 1993. A fascinating booklet detailing the present day Nelson connections in his home county.
Paul Davies. *The Battle of Trafalgar*. Pan books 1972. An informative paperback in the 'Panorama of History' series.
C. S. Forester. *Nelson, a biography*. An interesting account first published in 1929 by the man who subsequently wrote the famous Hornblower novels.
Thomas Hardy. *Nelson, Commemorative Medals 1797-1905*. The Nelson Society 1985. An extremely authoritative text on the subject.
David Howarth. *Trafalgar, The Nelson Touch*. Published by Collins 1969. An interesting and authoritative account of the Battle of Trafalgar.
Brian Lavery. *Nelson's Navy, The Ships, Men and Organisation 1793-1815*. Conway 1989. An absolutely indispensable handbook covering every aspect of the Navy in Nelson's time.
David Lyon. *The Navy Sailing List. All the Ships of the Royal Navy 1688-1860*. Conway 1993. A fine reference book resulting from years of research amongst the archives of the NMM.
Carola Oman. *Nelson*. First published in 1947 by Hodder & Stoughton. Since reprinted in several editions and regarded by many as the most authoritative modern biography.
Peter Padfield. *Nelson's War*. Granada 1976. A useful account of all the major actions involving Nelson.
Thomas Pocock. *Horatio Nelson*. Bodley Head 1987. One of the most recent biographies which includes a particularly useful list of primary sources.
Robert Southey. *The Life of Horatio Lord Nelson*. First published in 1813 and reprinted in many different editions since then. An early but very popular biography.

In addition to the foregoing, I have used numerous information booklets and leaflets published by the various museums mentioned in this book. Finally mention must be made of the interesting and informative *Nelson Dispatch*, the quarterly journal of the Nelson Society, presently running in its 5th volume and which often contains illuminating facts and commentary not found in other sources.

INTRODUCTION

Well, what is left of Nelson? The simple answer is — a staggering amount! At first glance the work entailed in the preparation of this book appeared to be quite straightforward. Some simple research at a few prominent museums would provide the background and a few exhibits could be catalogued. A visit to HMS *Victory* would provide some insight into life aboard his flagship and that would be that! How wrong can you be!

Although it is almost 200 years since Nelson was tragically struck down at the moment of his greatest triumph, there is still tremendous interest in, even controversy over, his life and achievements. Even when he was alive, he was recognised as the greatest naval tactician that the Royal Navy had ever produced and he was undoubtedly a born leader of men, inspiring his subordinates to great actions and achievements themselves. Set against this were personal traits which were the despair of his friends and provided ammunition for his detractors. His notorious affair with Emma Hamilton and his estrangement from his loyal wife were the talk of the country and he was certainly excluded from sections of the establishment and society because of that situation. As a person he was excessively vain, his attitude and obsessive display of his awards and decorations going far beyond a justifiable pride in his own achievements. Perhaps it is this combination of the brave, talented fighting commander and vain but naïve lover which has made Nelson such an enigmatic character and one which has attracted the attention and interest of people from all walks of life over the centuries.

In an age before telephones, radios, fax machines and all the other means of communications which we take for granted today, the handwritten word was the only way by which thoughts, ideas, orders, desires, hates or even dreams could be communicated between one person and another over any distance. Nelson was a prolific letter writer, even after the loss of his right arm in 1797, and at one time he commented that he was writing over 20 communications and letters a day. In most cases the recipients retained his letters and most have been preserved in one form or another, forming an enormous reservoir of information from which biographers have sought to build up a picture of the true man. Indeed there are probably more biographies of Nelson than of any other famous figure from England's illustrious past.

As he grew more famous, demand for illustrations of the man and his battles was almost insatiable. Many artists, some good and some bad, portrayed his likeness from life, and these paintings formed the basis of hundreds of engravings and prints which turn up today in museums, exhibitions, private collections, antique shops and even piles of junk. It was not only the man himself, but his battles, his associates, his lifestyle and even his death and grand funeral which all formed the subject of other prints and paintings. There were even cartoons, mostly extremely offensive even by the standards of today's tabloid press, directed at his relationship with Emma Hamilton and her husband, Sir William Hamilton.

Apart from words and pictures, there is a tremendous amount of actual material which belonged to Nelson or was closely associated with him. Again, as his fame increased, many people treasured and preserved such items and, following his death, his possessions were carefully gathered and retained by friends and relatives. For various reasons, many such items were relinquished and were bought, sold and exchanged so that now there is a bewildering array of Nelsonia for an enthusiast, researcher or collector to track down. Today, most major items are held in the collections of major museums but it is interesting to note that a significant proportion of items so held come from the efforts of two private collectors, both women. The Nelson Museum at Monmouth is based almost entirely on the collection built up around the turn of the century by Lady Llangattock, while the magnificent display in the Royal Naval Museum at Portsmouth is the work of a 20th century American collector, Mrs Lily Lambert McCarthy OBE. Merely to list all that is available or on view in these and other museums would more than fill a book of this size although an attempt has been made to describe those items of particular interest or significance. However, there will be plenty for the reader to discover by visiting the many establishments mentioned herein.

'Join the Navy and see the World' used to be a popular recruiting slogan, and it was never as true as in Nelson's day. With the exception of the Pacific Ocean and Australasia, Nelson's career took him to virtually every corner of the world and in many cases there are some recognisable features which can be associated with him or his activities. Some of these will be briefly described but, from a practical point of view, this book will concentrate on describing those places, mainly in the United Kingdom, where the reader can easily retrace the life of Nelson and get a feel for the places and buildings where he actually stood, ate, lived, talked, rested, suffered misfortunes or enjoyed happiness. And finally of course there is his quietly magnificent tomb in St Paul's Cathedral, and the profusion of monuments and memorials to commemorate his life and his victories in battle. These are scattered the length and breadth of the country and provide yet another link with the stirring past.

Despite the foregoing, in considering 'What's left of Nelson?', the most important legacy is the memory of the man — the Immortal Memory. In his own time he was an example and an inspiration not only to the men who served with him, but to the whole country, to the ordinary man and woman in the street. After his death, the idea of the 'Nelson Spirit', or the 'Nelson Touch', lived on strongly in the Royal Navy and even in two world wars was still a factor to inspire the fighting services and civilians in their efforts to defend their country. Today, the significance of a study of history is perhaps lost on the younger generation, many of whom would perhaps relate the name of Nelson to a South African politician rather than to Britain's most famous sailor. But even the original Nelson might have been proud of the man who was named after him and who perhaps drew some inspiration from the name and its associations with courage, firmness, tact, example and sacrifice.

In looking through this book and perhaps following up the information contained therein, the reader should try not to think of Nelson in terms of static museum exhibits, dusty documents or faintly interesting 18th century artefacts. Instead, stand back and try to imagine the boy playing in the Norfolk countryside, the young man learning his trade on the oceans of the world, the valiant and brilliant Captain risking life and limb in action, the human man so easily diverted by women, and finally as the inspirational Commander who fought and won some of history's most decisive naval battles, laying down his life at the moment of his greatest victory. It is in the mind and the memory that Nelson lives on, and will live on for all time, as an example and inspiration to all of us.

Below
Watercolour of Lady Llangattock at the Naval Temple, Monmouth 1905 (see page 157). *Nelson Museum, Monmouth*

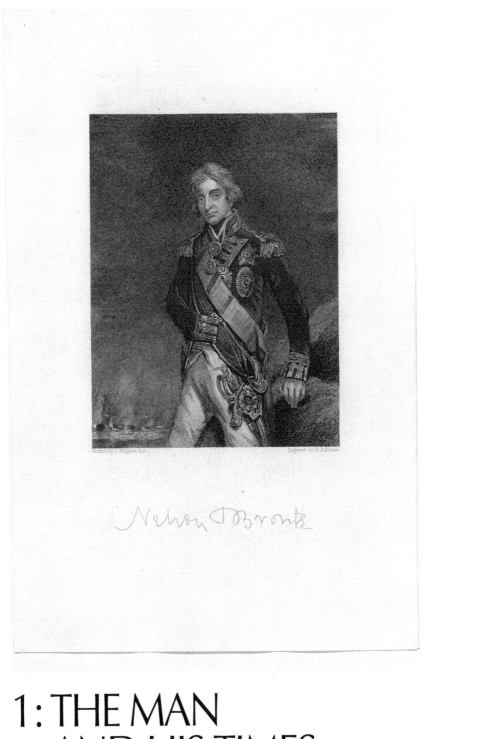

Nelson Bronte

1: THE MAN
AND HIS TIMES

Who was Nelson? What exactly did he do that has made him such a famous figure from the pages of history? Why, almost 200 years after his death does his name still have an evocative ring which stirs the imagination? In order to answer these questions it is essential to understand the world he lived in during the latter half of the 18th century and to briefly chart his career and experiences against that background.

Horatio Nelson was born in 1758 at a time when Europe was embroiled in the so-called Seven Years War. This was one of a series of wars fought in the 18th century as the European nations realised the importance of colonial development and the resulting trade and supply of raw materials which it brought. At the same time Britain, as an island nation, was sensitive to the power changes taking place along the coast of continental Europe, particularly the area of the Low Countries which today mostly consists of Belgium and the Netherlands. Thus the British obviously needed to defend their own colonial gains and also pursued a natural desire to increase these holdings wherever possible. At the same time there was an ever-present threat from a continental power which, if unchecked, could take over most of the European land mass and launch an invasion from the springboard formed by the Low Countries. In addition this area controlled access to the vital waterways of the Rhine, Scheldt and Maas which were the highways of the central European transportation system of the time. In the 18th century the prime enemy was France which variously succeeded in dominating large areas of Europe and constantly threatened an invasion of Britain while at the same time

possessing a large fleet to serve and protect its own colonial empire and to attack British possessions. For much of the period Spain was France's close ally, partly for political reasons and partly because of links between the respective monarchies.

The Seven Years War, often regarded as the most classic of colonial wars, ended in 1763 and in typical British fashion began with a few disasters but progressed to become a succession of spectacular victories against the French and Spanish forces. Quebec and much of Canada was captured, the French fleet was defeated in a major action off Quiberon Bay in 1759 and a Spanish fleet captured in Havana in 1762. At the end of the war the Royal Navy reigned supreme and a period of relative peace was established. However, there was intermittent fighting around the globe, particularly in the American colonies, which finally erupted into the War of American Independence in 1776. Although the colonial Americans had no fleet to speak of, they were soon supported by France and Spain so that another full scale naval war began and several battles were fought, notably the Battle of the Saintes where Admiral Rodney decisively defeated a French fleet in the West Indies in 1782. However, the war ended in the following year with Britain having lost its American colonies although it retained a considerable presence in Canada and the West Indies, not to mention the Indian empire on the other side of the world.

The War of Independence was the last of the wars fought almost solely for colonial and trade reasons, since developments in France completely changed the motivations of both sides and threatened the very existence of Britain and its way of life. In 1789 the French Revolution, one of the great turning points in history, broke out and eventually swept away the French Monarchy amid the revolting bloodbath of the guillotine and the 'Reign of Terror'. Alarmed that revolutionary fervour should gain a hold in Britain, the government joined an alliance which included Austria, Prussia, Spain and Naples in a war against the French revolutionary forces. It is perhaps difficult to envisage Europe as it was at that time; Austria and its Hungarian empire was a major power and the modern concept of Germany did not exist. Nor did Italy, although the Kingdom of Naples encompassed much of what is today southern Italy, as well as the island of Sicily.

Unfortunately for Britain, most of her allies' military strength melted away in the face of the nationalistic and ideologically motivated French Army and by 1797 she was standing alone against the combined forces of France, Spain and Holland, while the Royal Navy had ignominiously completely withdrawn from the Mediterranean. However, the blackest hour lies before the dawn, and by the end of the year the situation was improving. Under Admiral Sir John Jervis the Royal Navy defeated a combined French and Spanish fleet in the Atlantic off Cape St Vincent and it was in this battle that Nelson was first thrown into prominence, winning a knighthood for his actions in capturing two large Spanish ships, thus enabling the other British ships to engage and defeat the remainder. Later in the year Admiral Duncan defeated the Dutch fleet at Camperdown and in 1798 Nelson, now a Rear-Admiral, gained a famous and decisive victory in the Battle of the Nile — forever ending Napoleon's dreams of an eastward expansion of his empire.

It was partly as a result of this defeat that Napoleon turned his attentions to the remainder of continental Europe and, as his armies spread across the map, the Baltic states of Denmark, Sweden and Russia formed an 'armed neutrality' in the hope of warding off the potential threat from the French by keeping Britain out of the Baltic. However, Britain could not accept this situation as she needed access to the Baltic trade, particularly in items such as tar, hemp and timber which were so vital to the building and maintenance of her naval fleet. It was for this reason that Nelson, under Admiral Sir Hyde Parker, was dispatched to the Baltic and subsequently defeated the Danish fleet at the hard-fought Battle of Copenhagen.

Meanwhile a change of government at home led to a movement for peace and the Treaty of Amiens was signed in March 1802. Although Napoleon continued with his continental conquests, the British forces were rapidly demobilised and many of the Navy's ships laid up or neglected. But peace did not last long and war broke out again the following year with events moving rapidly to a climax. Napoleon declared himself Emperor and the French Army made obvious and massive preparations to invade Britain across the Channel. While the French Navy was incapable of securing widespread control of the seas, it was large enough (especially when combined with the Spanish fleet) to secure command of the English Channel long enough for a successful invasion to take place. The resulting cat and mouse naval campaign as the French and Spanish fleets manoeuvred to draw the British fleet away from the Channel while they concentrated their own forces for the invasion resulted in one of the greatest sea chases ever and led Nelson out of the Mediterranean and right across the Atlantic and back before battle was eventually joined at Trafalgar in October 1805.

The result was a glorious British victory which effectively ended French seapower as a factor in the war and provided the basis for almost a century when the Royal Navy was the undisputed master of the world's seas and oceans. Nelson himself was struck down in the heat of the battle, but died knowing that a famous victory had been won. The wars dragged on for another 10 years before Napoleon was finally defeated at Waterloo in 1815 but it was significant that

CAPTAIN MAURICE SUCKLING. R.N.

Ridley sculp.

after fleeing the battlefield he finally surrendered to a ship of the Royal Navy which had been so instrumental in his downfall. The revolutionary wars which raged from 1793 to 1815 were truly worldwide in their scope, just as much as the two world wars in this century. After 1815 there was a long period of relative peace in which Britain was the major power in the world and in which the modern world as we know it today evolved. That this happened was a direct result of the outcome of the wars, which in turn rested firmly on the achievements of British seapower and its climax at Trafalgar in 1805.

Thus, the time in which Nelson lived was one of almost continuous war and it was natural that any boy with a spirit of adventure would end up fighting for his country. But his early years at Burnham Thorpe, a small and quiet village in Norfolk, were little different to those of any child of the time. His father was the Reverend Edmund Nelson who was appointed to All Saints' church in 1755 and the family lived in a rambling rectory some three-quarters of a mile away from the church. Here Horatio Nelson was born, the sixth of 11 children although by the time of his birth two of his elder brothers had already died from childhood ailments leaving only two brothers, William and Maurice, and a sister, Susannah. After Horatio came Anne, Edmund, Suckling (his mother's maiden name), George and Catherine. With all these children around, as well as others in the village, the young Horatio would not have lacked for company. He attended local schools at Norwich and North Walsham, and at an early age showed an interest in playing with toy boats and water. Perhaps the proximity of the River Burn, flowing past the rectory, was a factor in this but in fact the sea was not far away and the two or three miles to the tidal creek at Overy Staithe could quickly be covered on foot or on horseback.

Nelson's mother, of whom he appears to have had fond memories, died in 1767 leaving the Rector with eight children to bring up (a younger brother, George, having died in 1766) and this was a most difficult task as money was short. However, relatives rallied round and efforts were made to find openings for the children. Maurice, the eldest brother left, aged 15, to work as a clerk in London while Susannah, the oldest child, went to work as an apprentice milliner in Bath. Horatio himself expressed a desire to join the Navy, spurred on perhaps by the announcement in late 1770 that his uncle, Captain Maurice Suckling, was commissioning the *Raisonnable*, a 64-gun ship-of-the-line. His uncle's comment on hearing this has been often quoted but bears repeating here,

'What has poor Horace done, who is so weak, that above all the rest he should be sent to rough it out at sea? But let him come; and the first time we go into action, a cannon ball may knock off his head, and provide for him at once'. It is interesting to note that the young Nelson was known as Horace, a name which he appears to have preferred himself in his early years, and also to catch the implication that his health was not too good. Indeed Nelson's life and career were plagued by ill health and he was never physically strong, despite which he was always active and managed to recover from several serious wounds.

His introduction to the Navy in January 1770 at the age of 12 was not auspicious. With some difficulty he made his way to Chatham where nobody met him and he could not find his ship. Although he eventually managed to board the *Raisonnable*, it was only to find that nobody was expecting him and that his uncle was away. Friendless and ignored, he was left to his own devices for some time before anyone even spoke to him but eventually things were sorted out and he settled down to life as a midshipman aboard one of His Majesty's Ships of War. However, this did not last long as the *Raisonnable*, which had been commissioned in the expectation of a war with Spain, was paid off as the threat receded and Captain Suckling was appointed to command HMS *Triumph 74* which was acting as the Thames guardship, a static duty which offered little scope for an energetic young midshipman. Accordingly his uncle arranged for the young Nelson to join a merchant vessel making a voyage to the West Indies and return. The ship's master was a Mr John Rathbone who had previously been master's mate on the *Dreadnought* and was entrusted with the task of teaching the young lad all he knew about navigation and seamanship. On his return to England Nelson rejoined HMS *Triumph* and was entrusted with the command of the ship's cutter and long boat, learning much in the process about the piloting of craft in shoal and tidal waters.

In 1773 the government decided to launch a naval expedition to explore the possibility of a North East passage through the Arctic seas to the Pacific Ocean and commissioned two converted bomb ketches, *Racehorse* and *Carcass*, for the purpose. The expedition would also carry civilian scientists to observe and report on the findings of the expedition into the unknown Arctic seas. As the ships were prepared at Deptford on the upper reaches of the Thames, Nelson decided on his own initiative to try and join the expedition. Despite an official Admiralty order that no boys were to form any part of the crews, he successfully persuaded Captain Lutwidge of the *Carcass* to take him along, ostensibly as coxswain of the Captain's gig — an early example of Nelson's zeal and

Opposite:
Captain Maurice Suckling was Nelson's uncle and started the young lad on his naval career aboard the *Raisonable* in 1771.
National Maritime Museum

Left:
A painting of the oft told incident involving Nelson and a Polar bear which occurred during the 1773 Arctic expedition. This is one of a series of paintings by Richard Westall depicting episodes from Nelson's life which can be seen at Greenwich *National Maritime Museum.*

determination. The expedition itself achieved little, reaching the icefields north of Spitzbergen by the end of July, already late in the season. The ships became icebound and, for a while, it looked as if they would have to be abandoned, leaving the crews to haul the ships' boats over the ice to open waters for a hazardous voyage back to civilisation. It was during this period that Nelson was observed squaring up without fear to a polar bear on the ice, hoping to shoot it with a rather ineffectual handgun so that he could take the fur skin home to his father. Fortunately his Captain ordered a cannon to be discharged, frightening the bear which ran off. As preparations proceeded to evacuate the ships, a north-easterly wind blew up and dislodged the ice field, enabling the ships to regain open water, albeit with some difficulty, and they eventually returned safely to England at the end of September.

Nelson lost no time in obtaining an appointment to another ship, this time the 24-gun frigate *Seahorse* commanded by Captain George Farmer and about to set off for the East Indies. By October he was at sea again, rated as a midshipman, and spent the following two and a half years visiting almost every part of the East Indies before being struck down with a serious fever which temporarily paralysed him and caused him to be transferred to the frigate *Dolphin* for passage home. It was during this six month voyage, as he lay barely conscious in his bunk, it is reputed that he had a vision of a 'golden orb' which gave him a glimpse of his future and became a source of inspiration to him. Certainly by the time he reached England in August 1776 he was well enough to accept an appointment to HMS *Worcester* (64 guns) sailing with a convoy to Gibraltar. By this time the American War of Independence had broken out but, nevertheless, Nelson's appointment was undoubtedly due to the influence of his uncle, Captain Suckling, who was now Comptroller of the Navy, in charge of the Navy Board. This important post was responsible for the building, maintenance and arming of ships, and its holder exercised considerable power and influence — fortunately for Nelson.

On his return from Gibraltar, Nelson underwent the compulsory examination for promotion to Lieutenant on 9 April 1777, having held acting rank aboard the *Worcester*. Although his uncle was chairman of the examining board, he did not reveal this connection until the young candidate had successfully answered all the questions thrown at him. Afterwards Captain Suckling said that he did not wish his nephew to be unduly favoured as he had confidently expected the lad to pass on his own merits, as indeed happened. The following day Nelson was appointed as Second Lieutenant to the frigate *Lowestoft 32* commanded by Captain William Locker and which was fitting out for duties on the West Indies station. It turned out to be a particularly happy time for Nelson who struck up an immediate rapport with his new Captain and with whom in later life he maintained a regular correspondence which has proved of much use to historians. Once in the West Indies the *Lowestoft* was soon in action with American privateers and by the end of the year Nelson was given his first independent command, a captured schooner renamed *Little Lucy* after Captain Locker's daughter.

In the spring of 1778 Admiral Sir Peter Parker took over as Commander-in-Chief Jamaica and Nelson was transferred, with warm recommendations by Captain Locker, to his flagship *HMS Bristol 50* as Third Lieutenant although by September he had become First Lieutenant. At the end of the year he was appointed as Commander to the brig *Badger* and after some action in the Bay of Honduras he distinguished himself by organising the rescue of the crew of the *Glasgow*, a 20-gun Sixth Rate, which caught fire while lying in Montego Bay. His actions were soon rewarded when he was promoted to the rank of Post Captain and given command of the 28-gun frigate *Hinchingbroke* whose previous captain had been killed in action. Although this promotion was well-deserved and earned, there was an element of luck in the timing as Nelson's influential uncle, Captain Suckling, had recently died and he could expect no further assistance in his career from that source. Nevertheless, aged only 21, Nelson was now at the foot of the career ladder which eventually and inevitably would take him to flag rank and the chance of fame and fortune.

Engraved by H. Robinson.

SAMUEL, FIRST VISCOUNT HOOD.

OB. 1816.

FROM THE ORIGINAL OF SIR J. REYNOLDS, IN THE COLLECTION OF

THE RIGHT HON.^{BLE} THE VISCOUNTESS BRIDPORT.

However, things did not go well for a while. As the *Hinchingbroke* was away, he was temporarily given command of the port defences at Kingston as a French fleet threatened to invade the island. After the scare passed, Nelson joined his new ship in September to set off in support of an ill-conceived expedition to send troops up the San Juan river to attack Spanish forts in Nicaragua. Although Nelson's task was merely to escort and convey the troops to the mouth of the river, with typical zeal and determination he stayed with the expedition and was instrumental in assisting the troops to move upstream for almost 70 miles through thick tropical rain forest. Although the forts were eventually taken, the cost in men was horrendous and no more than 10 (!) out of *Hinchingbroke's* crew of 200 survived to tell the tale, the rest dying from disease, probably malaria. Nelson himself, recalled to Jamaica before the forts were taken, was again seriously ill and laid low with a fever. He recovered slightly and took command of a 44-gun frigate, HMS *Janus*, but almost immediately suffered a serious relapse and eventually was forced to return to England at the end of 1780 for a period of convalescence, staying in Bath for several months.

Towards the end of 1781 he was well enough to take command of the 28-gun frigate *Albermarle*, a captured French merchantman with poor sailing qualities which had been converted to a frigate. Nevertheless, Nelson was determined to make the best of his new ship although his first task was escorting a convoy to the Baltic as winter approached, a stark contrast to his previous three years in the tropics. However, in the spring of 1782 he was ordered across the Atlantic to the North American station and, while on patrol off the Massachusetts coast, had a narrow escape when pursued by four French sail-of-the-line and a frigate. With great skill he manoeuvred his ship into shoal waters where the French dared not follow and they eventually withdrew. On the same cruise his crew began to experience serious symptoms of scurvy, not having taken on fresh provisions for over five months. Returning up the St Lawrence to Quebec, the seriously ill were taken ashore to hospital and the *Albermarle* remained there for over a month while they recuperated. Nelson had learned a valuable lesson and was thereafter meticulous in ensuring that the crews of ships under his command always received adequate fresh provisions.

His stay in Quebec was also punctuated by a romantic entanglement, to which Nelson seemed particularly prone. The lady in question, one Mary Simpson, was the daughter of one of the garrison's officers and when Nelson was eventually ordered to sail he was only persuaded with great difficulty not to abandon his naval career so that he could stay in Canada and, presumably marry Miss Simpson. The man responsible for changing his mind was Alexander Davison, a military agent and contractor who was to become a great personal friend of Nelson. After leaving Quebec, the *Albermarle* met up with a fleet under Lord Hood who was impressed enough with the young Captain Nelson to allow him to accompany his fleet when it returned to the West Indies. At this time Nelson also met Prince William, the future Duke of Clarence and King William IV, who was serving on Hood's ships as a midshipman. However, the cruise in the West Indies proved fruitless and the *Albermarle* returned to Portsmouth to pay off in June 1783.

With the end of the War of Independence, there was no prospect of immediate employment and Nelson elected to spend some time in France, partly to save money and partly to try and learn the language. He does not appear to have been very successful at either but, once again, fell in love, this time with the daughter of an English clergyman living in St Omer on the Channel coast. However, he returned to England early in 1784 and in March was appointed to command the 28-gun frigate *Boreas*, and once again was soon bound for the West Indies. This commission lasted for

Opposite:
The earliest authenticated portrait of Nelson was painted by Francis Rigaud and shows him as a recently promoted Captain in 1781. It shows a rather likeable, if earnest, young man. *National Maritime Museum*

Previous page:
Samuel, Lord Hood, came from an illustrious naval family and, as an Admiral, met Nelson when serving on the American station in 1782. Thereafter he did much to encourage Nelson's career before he retired in 1795. *Author's Collection*

over three years and it was July 1787 before he saw Portsmouth again. In the meantime Nelson once more demonstrated himself to be an efficient and zealous officer — perhaps too zealous as his attempts to enforce the Navigation Laws which prevented the use of American vessels for trading in the Leeward Islands did not meet with the approval of the local business community. During this time he cemented what was to be a lifelong friendship with Cuthbert Collingwood who was also commanding a frigate, and he also became a friend and confidant of Prince William who was now also commanding a ship of his own.

However, the most significant relationship to be formed was with an attractive young widow, Frances Nisbet, who was the daughter of the President of Nevis and the mother of a young boy by her earlier marriage. Nelson was instantly attracted to her and after an 18-month engagement, most of which he spent at sea, they were duly married at Montpelier on the island of Nevis on Sunday 11 March 1787. Almost immediately Nelson sailed for home in the *Boreas*, leaving his new bride to follow a few months later in a merchantman. England was now at peace and for the next five years Nelson was unemployed and spent most of his time with his wife in the rectory at Burnham Thorpe. Used to the warm tropics, his new wife, Fanny, found the bleak Norfolk winters a trial while Nelson fretted at his inactivity, made harder by his small income of eight shillings a day that represented the half pay of a naval captain with no ship. It was not a happy time for either of them.

Although Nelson made several attempts to gain a new appointment, he appeared to have little influence at the Admiralty and it is possible that he was regarded as being somewhat overzealous as a result of his activities in support of the Navigation Laws in the West Indies. However, the outbreak of the French Revolutionary Wars in 1793 at last brought this frustrating period to an end and he was overjoyed to be offered the command of a 64-gun ship-of-the-line, the *Agamemnon*. This appointment really marked the turning point in his life and from now on he was to be almost continually in action or in a position of high command, and was to perform the many heroic deeds upon which his reputation today is founded.

Nelson took the *Agamemnon* to sea early in 1793 and joined a fleet under Admiral Lord Hood destined for the Mediterranean. By midsummer the ships were closely blockading the French port of Toulon which was subsequently taken over by French Royalists and occupied by British troops. Nelson was dispatched to Naples to persuade the King of Naples and the Two Sicilies to send more troops as reinforcements. Although only staying a few days, he was successful in his mission but, more significantly, he met for the first time the British Envoy, Sir William Hamilton and his young wife, Emma — two people who were later to become inextricably tangled with his life and career. After returning to Toulon, he was again detached from the main fleet and on 22 October the *Agamemnon* became engaged in a running fight with several French ships including four frigates. This was Nelson's first major action and he acquitted himself well although the faster French ships eventually escaped, but not before one frigate was reduced to almost a wreck.

In the meantime, the British forces and their allies had been forced to abandon Toulon and the city had been retaken by French Revolutionary forces in December 1793 assisted by some extremely effective artillery under the command of a Lt-Col Bonaparte. With Toulon lost, the British urgently needed a new base in the Mediterranean and the island of Corsica seemed the best choice, particularly as many of the islanders already resented French rule. The first objective was the town of Bastia in the north of the island and this was captured after a siege by a force of marines and seamen under Nelson's command. The next objective was Calvi on the north-western shore and although this was a joint Army/Navy operation, the situation was much more difficult. The initial landings were made in June 1794 and a month later Nelson was ashore directing the fire of a battery of guns landed from the *Agamemnon* when he was hit in the face by stones and gravel thrown up from an exploding shell. As a result he permanently lost the sight of his right eye although, typically, he shrugged it off and continued with his duties aboard ship and Calvi fell to the British forces in the August.

For some reason Nelson's activities and leadership during the Corsica campaign were never officially recognised or rewarded and indeed, many years later he had a little difficulty in obtaining the pension to which he was entitled as a result of his wound! However, he was not left to brood on this situation and in March the following year took part in his first full fleet action when he was part of a British force under Admiral

Opposite:
A rare portrait of Lady Nelson, née Francis Nisbet. The artist is unknown. *National Maritime Museum*

Left:
A contemporary view of Bastia, on the island of Corsica, where Nelson led a naval force to capture the town. *National Maritime Museum*

Hotham which engaged 15 French sail-of-the-line off the coast of Genoa. The *Agamemnon*, being a good sailer, pulled ahead of the other British ships and engaged the *Ça Ira*, an 80-gun French ship supported by two others including the 120-gun *Sans Culotte*. After reducing the enemy ship to a battered wreck, Nelson was ordered to disengage, but the next day the *Ça Ira* was captured while under tow although the rest of the French fleet was allowed to escape as Hotham decided not to press his advantage. A few months later, in July 1795, Nelson was in command of an inshore squadron consisting of the *Agamemnon* and several frigates when he was involved in another major fleet action (the Battle of Hyères) under Admiral Hotham but again the result was inconclusive.

Early in 1796, still in command of the inshore squadron which now included no less than eight frigates, Nelson was officially appointed Commodore but another appointment was to have a greater significance. The ineffective Admiral Hotham was replaced as C-in-C Mediterranean by Admiral Sir John Jervis, a vigorous man with a high professional reputation. Nelson established an immediate rapport with his new commander who was keen to retain his services in the Mediterranean but his ship, the *Agamemnon*, was by now in urgent need of a refit and had to be sent home. Nelson was given command of the 74-gun HMS *Captain* and hoisted his broad Commodore's pennant aboard her on 11 June 1796. However, the next few months were depressing as the Navy was forced to turn to one of its traditional activities, evacuating civilians and troops from various points on the Genoan and Italian coast as the unstoppable French army swept across northern Italy. Eventually Corsica was also evacuated and in December 1796 Nelson temporarily hoisted his flag aboard the frigate *Minerve 38* and with another, *Blanche*, in company set out from Gibraltar to evacuate the last of the British garrison from the island of Elba. Five days later they ran into two Spanish frigates one of which was dismasted and captured. However, the following day a more powerful Spanish force including two ships-of-the-line came into view and the *Minerve* was forced to cast off her prize and eventually managed to escape during the night. Not content with all this action, Nelson and the *Minerve* then captured a small French privateer off Sardinia before eventually reaching Elba. At the end of January he set sail again for Gibraltar but whilst on passage learnt that the Spanish fleet had sailed from Cartagena, heading for the Atlantic. Fearing that he might miss a major fleet action, Nelson pressed on with all speed and was soon being chased by three Spanish ships as he left Gibraltar. As all sail was pressed on there was a call of 'man overboard' and Nelson's Lieutenant, an officer called Hardy (of whom more anon!), took charge of a jolly boat lowered to search unsuccessfully for the lost seaman. By this time the Spanish ships were drawing fast on the scene but Nelson shortened sail and hove to, enabling the jolly boat to be picked up. Surprisingly the Spanish ships also hove to, perhaps suspecting some trap, and Nelson's luck held as he wore away again to the west.

After nightfall, a thick fog crept over the sea and Nelson's luck was pushed even further as he found himself sailing through the middle of the Spanish fleet! Fortunately he was not observed and the next morning he came upon the British fleet under Admiral Jervis and was able to return on board the *Captain*. He was just in time as one of the major sea battles of the war was now about to be fought and Nelson was at last to have the opportunity to show his true worth and courage in circumstances which would bring him rewards and recognition. In what was to be typical Nelson fashion he made the most of the opportunity.

The situation on the morning of 14 February 1797 was that the British fleet of 15 ships-of-the-line supported by four frigates was in a position to intercept the Spanish Grand Fleet of 27 sail-of-the-line accompanied by 10 frigates off Cape St Vincent, some 150 miles north-west of Cadiz. Even these numbers do not indicate the full superiority of the Spanish force which included six 112-gun three deckers as well as the four decked 136-gun *Santissima Trinidad*, the largest warship in the world at that time. The British fleet included only six three-deckers and the two largest (*Victory* and *Britannia*) only mounted 100 guns. Almost all the rest were standard 74s. As the enemy ships sailed steadily eastwards towards Cadiz, Jervis signalled his ships, sailing south in line ahead, to aim to pass through a gap which was developing between the leading group of nine Spanish ships and the remainder which were beginning to trail behind in an untidy bunch. As the British ships, led by the *Culloden 74*, passed through the Spanish line the enemy turned away to port in an attempt to pass behind the British line. Jervis ordered his ships to tack in succession which meant that the *Culloden* would reverse course, followed in turn by each following ship as it reached the same point. Nelson, aboard the *Captain*, was near the rear of the British line and as the battle developed he realised that by the time the *Culloden* had led the British ships back to the scene of the battle, the main body of Spanish ships would have passed behind them and the result would be a long chase, with the odds in favour of the Spaniards making good their escape on a fair wind.

In order to prevent this Nelson turned out of the line and reversed course, throwing his ship in the path of the advancing Spanish ships, led by the mighty *Santissima Trinidad*. In the context of the time this action was incredible on several counts, not the least of which was the physical courage required to place his ship, unsupported, amongst the might of the enemy ships. However, it took even more courage to break out of the line on his own initiative in direct contravention of the orders of his commanding Admiral. Other officers had been court martialled and severely punished for lesser transgressions and the ethos of the time did not encourage the display of initiative by junior officers. However, Jervis was quick to realise the significance of Nelson's actions and ordered the *Excellent*, another 74 commanded by Nelson's friend Collingwood and bringing up the rear of the British line, to follow Nelson and support him. Soon afterwards the *Culloden* bore up, followed by the *Blenheim* and for a while these ships took the brunt of the action until the remaining British ships could turn and catch up, a manoeuvre which took some time in a ponderous sailing ship. After almost an hour of desperate fighting the *Captain* was almost totally dismasted and virtually unsteerable and Nelson ordered her to be laid alongside the 80-gun *San Nicolas* which was also badly

Below:
An old engraving depicting the *Captain* alongside the *San Nicolas* and *San Josef* at the Battle of St Vincent.
National Maritime Museum

damaged and had become entangled with the three-decker *San Josef* of 112 guns. As the ships crashed together Nelson led a boarding party from the fore chains of the *Captain* into the quarter gallery of the *San Nicolas*, entering through a smashed window and making his way through the cabin to the quarterdeck where other British seaman, marines and soldiers had already gained control.

As the dispirited Spanish officers began to surrender, there was a volley of musket fire from the decks of the *San Josef* which towered above them alongside. Nelson at once organised another boarding party and without hesitation leapt across to the other ship, shouting 'Westminster Abbey or glorious Victory!'. This rush was too much for the crew of the *San Josef* which had already been severely mauled by fire from other British ships, notably the 98-gun *Prince George*, and resistance quickly crumbled. There then occurred an amazing scene as Nelson walked the deck of the conquered ship, accepting the surrendered swords of the vanquished officers and passing them to one of his seamen who nonchalantly tucked them under his arm as a lady-in-waiting would collect up bunches of flowers proffered to the Queen on a modern walkabout.

By this time the rest of the action was also coming to an end and the defeated Spanish fleet, with several of their ships crippled, made off in the fading light, leaving the British in possession of four captured ships including the *San Josef* and *San Nicolas*. As a result of this action Nelson sprang to prominence in the eyes of the British people and he was rewarded with the conferring of a knighthood, the Order of the Bath. Coincidentally he also received news of his promotion to Rear-Admiral of the Blue, although this had actually been gazetted a few days before the battle as a result of normal seniority. Admiral Jervis was honoured with a peerage, becoming an Earl and taking the title St Vincent. Nelson's action in capturing a Spanish first rate by boarding it via an intermediate enemy ship was unprecedented in naval history and was popularly referred to as 'Nelson's Patent Bridge for boarding First Rates'!

Back at Gibraltar Nelson and his flag captain, Captain Miller, eventually transferred to the *Theseus*, a 74 newly arrived from England. However, this was an extremely unhappy ship with the crew on the verge of mutiny but, together, Nelson and Miller set out to right the men's grievances and to make sure that the ship's stores were fully replenished. Within a fortnight a profound change had come over the ship and a handwritten note, surreptitiously dropped on the deck where it would be found and passed to the Admiral, read as follows:

'Success attend Admiral Nelson! God Bless Captain Miller. We thank them for the officers they have placed over us. We are happy and comfortable, and will shed every drop of blood in our veins, and the name of Theseus shall be immortalised as high as the Captain's.' It was signed *'Ship's Company'.*

Although a relatively minor event in Nelson's career, it illustrates once again his concern for the men serving under him and the enthusiasm and loyalty with which he was repaid. It was not long before the crew had a chance to prove their claims as the *Theseus* joined the rest of the British fleet in a blockade of the Spanish fleet at Cadiz. Disappointed at the reluctance of the Spanish ships to come out and fight, it was decided to launch an attack and bombardment on the town. One of the bomb ketches, the *Thunderer*, was hit and disabled, tempting several enemy small craft and gunboats to come out in an attempt to capture her. Several British launches were immediately dispatched to assist the *Thunderer* and among these was Nelson in his barge manned by 10 men and his coxswain, John Sykes. During the fierce action Nelson's boat was attacked by the Spanish commander's barge carrying almost 30 officers and men. In the savage hand-to-hand combat which followed, Nelson was twice saved by the heroic actions of his coxswain who shielded the Admiral with his own body, taking serious wounds in the process. Eventually the Spanish barge surrendered with every crewman either dead or wounded and once again Nelson had seemed to lead a charmed life as he led his men in battle, always at the point of the hottest action.

A few days later he was summoned to St Vincent's flagship and given fresh orders, to lead a force of ships and men against the port of Santa Cruz on the Spanish-held island of Tenerife. The object was the capture of the port and the destruction of its defences, together with the taking of various merchant ships believed to be carrying valuable cargoes. Once again it was an entirely naval expedition, the landing force being made up of marines and sailors carried by a fleet which included several 74s and three frigates. The result was a bloody disaster and Nelson himself was lucky to escape with his life. It had been hoped to make a surprise dawn landing to the north-east of the town by a force which would then scale the heights to capture gun batteries commanding the town and anchorage. The frigates would then come close inshore to support a further assault on the town itself. Almost immediately the plan ran into trouble when the first landings were delayed by unexpectedly strong winds and tides,

Opposite:
Nelson receives the swords of the defeated Spanish Admiral and other officers aboard the *San Josef. National Maritime Museum*

Above:
An engraving of Nelson produced in 1787 after the Battle of St Vincent and based on Rigaud's earlier portrait. On display at the Bucklers Hard Maritime Museum. *ASM*

and all surprise was lost. A subsequent landing achieved little and all forces were re-embarked and deployed for a desperate frontal attack on the city which took place on the night of Monday 24 July 1797. Nelson himself, never one to order his men to carry out anything he was not prepared to do himself, accompanied a group of boats attempting to storm and capture the harbour mole. At the instant he stepped ashore, in the act of drawing his sword, he was hit in the right arm as several other men around him fell in a hail of grapeshot.

There is no doubt that he subsequently owed his life to the prompt actions of his stepson, Josiah Nisbet, who found him lying on the stone quay and quickly had him carried back to a boat. With the help of five other men and with great difficulty, he got the boat back into the water and had it rowed out to the fleet waiting offshore. Nelson's shattered arm was bandaged and a tourniquet applied to stem the loss of blood. Despite the severity of the wound, he was conscious and insisted on being carried back to his flagship, *Theseus*, despite the proximity of other ships, and he also ordered that the boat stop to pick up survivors from another sunken boat so that it was almost an hour before he came alongside. He then insisted on boarding his flagship unaided and then went below where the assistant surgeon, M. Ronicet (a Frenchman!) performed the inevitable amputation.

Ashore, things were going from bad to worse and with many of the landing force drowned or killed in the initial assault, the remainder under Captain Troubridge were surrounded in the centre of the town. In a gesture of defiance, Troubridge threatened to burn the town if his force was not permitted to withdraw unharmed, a request granted by the chivalrous governor of the Canaries who also provided fresh provisions for the British Fleet and assistance with the care of the wounded — wars were fought differently in those days! Nevertheless, the British force had been soundly repulsed and Nelson, although remaining active despite the loss of his arm, was extremely depressed and assumed that his naval career was at an end, an opinion he expressed to St Vincent when he rejoined the rest of the British fleet off Cadiz. St Vincent himself thought otherwise and apportioned no blame to Nelson in respect of the events which had occurred.

Nelson returned to England aboard the frigate *Seahorse* and arrived at Portsmouth on 1 September, subsequently travelling to Bath were he was reunited with his wife and father. After a few days he moved to London where he stayed for several weeks, recuperating from his wound which continued to cause great pain and suffering until the end of November when the silk ligature which had been used to bind the wound eventually came away, allowing the scarred tissue to heal finally. By the beginning of December he was in a cheerful mood and had been appointed as Rear Admiral of the Blue to the Mediterranean fleet to serve again under St Vincent, his flagship being the *Vanguard 74,* newly out of drydock and commanded by the newly promoted Captain

Berry, Nelson's former first lieutenant aboard the Captain. Leaving England early in April 1798, he sailed to join St Vincent and was immediately given command of a squadron consisting of three 74s and four frigates, with orders to enter the Mediterranean and observe the movements of the powerful French fleet based at Toulon.

He soon learned that Bonaparte was at Toulon with an army of 40,000 men in the process of embarking aboard a fleet of merchant and troopships which would be escorted by a force of at least 15 ships-of-the-line, although their objectives and destination were as yet unknown. While patrolling off the French coast, his flagship was severely damaged and dismasted in a storm and the ship was saved only by the efforts and seamanship of Captain Ball of the *Alexander* who took the stricken ship in tow and clawed her off a lee shore and its threatening rocks. However, the ship was miraculously repaired within four days and Nelson resumed his duties, now reinforced by a further 10 ships-of-the-line sent by St Vincent together with instructions to hunt down the French fleet and destroy it. Unfortunately the French force, under the command of Admiral de Brueys had sailed while Nelson's ships were becalmed off Sardinia, and their destination was unknown. Nelson was severely handicapped by a lack of frigates which were needed to cover the many parts of the Mediterranean which might constitute the French objective and so he was forced to fall back on a certain amount of guesswork. In fact he made a brilliant, and exactly correct, deduction that the probable destination was Egypt with the objective of defeating the powerful Turkish empire and opening the way for an attack on the British possessions in the Indian subcontinent. In typical Nelson fashion, the British fleet pressed all sail and made a speedy passage to Alexandria — where there was no sign of the French fleet. Nelson had been entirely correct in his assumptions but his fleet of experienced Royal Navy ships had made a much faster passage than the French, encumbered by the vast slow moving troop convoy, and he had in fact overtaken them, twice passing within a few miles of the enemy which had been hidden by bad weather or darkness. Disappointed, Nelson set sail to search, along the coast of Turkey and then back to Syracuse, for nearly a month before finally receiving news that Alexandria after all had been the French objective. The British fleet immediately sailed south again and arrived off the Egyptian port on the afternoon of 1 August 1798, after a chase which had lasted almost two months.

By this time the French Army had disembarked and was well established ashore, but the ships-of-the-line were moored close together in a long line in the shallow waters of Aboukir Bay where de Brueys thought them safe from attack. The 13 sail-of-the-line included the flagship *L'Orient* of 120 guns, three 80-gun ships and nine 74s as well as

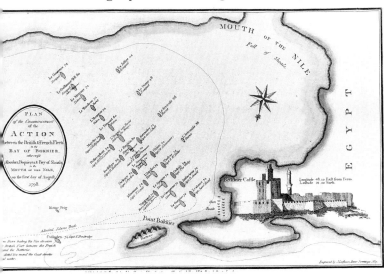

Opposite:
The Battle of the Nile reaches its climax as the French flagship *L'Orient* burns fiercely before blowing up. *National Maritime Museum*

Left:
A contemporary plan of the Battle of the Nile showing the disposition of the French fleet in Aboukir Bay. The plan also shows the British ships which have sailed close under the lee of the island before turning to lie on either side of the enemy line. *National Maritime Museum*

four frigates while at the commencement of the action Nelson could only muster 10 74s, the 50 gun *Leander* and the brig *Mutine* (commanded by a young officer called Hardy). As Nelson's ships approached, it was late afternoon and de Brueys confidently expected that he would have the night to prepare for battle as no sensible commander would be expected to risk his ships in the shoal waters in darkness and without access to accurate charts or pilots. Nelson, however, had no such inhibition and, after ordering dinner to be served, he continued to press on towards the bay. The French had literally been caught with their pants down and made frenzied efforts to recall men from ashore and their ships tried to clear for action. Most only cleared the guns on the seaward side as it was assumed that there was no room for any British ships to pass inside them, so close to the shallows were they anchored.

Meanwhile Nelson, having finished his dinner, made only three flag signals which were to prepare for battle, to get ready to anchor by the stern and to engage the enemy's van and centre. No other orders were necessary as he had often and thoroughly discussed with all his captains what tactics would be required and used in every conceivable type of engagement so that when the moment came, there was no need for detailed or confusing signals. This was becoming one of Nelson's trademarks and one of the major factors contributing to his success as a commander. Bristling with confidence and expectation the British ships continued to bear down on the enemy and the action commenced at 6.28pm as the French opened fire on the leading British ship, the *Goliath*. Commanded by Thomas Foley, the *Goliath* surprised the French by passing under the bows of the *Le Guerrier*, raking her with a broadside as she did so, and then sailing inside the French line. Within a few minutes there were four other British ships inside the French line, each preparing to anchor alongside a French ship and batter it into submission. Nelson's flagship, the *Vanguard*, passed outside the line and anchored almost alongside the *Le Spartiate*, third in the French line, followed by the rest of the British ships as they came up. Far behind

Above:
Naples as it would have appeared to Nelson. The bay is dominated by Mount Vesuvius, visible in the background.
Author's Collection

was the *Culloden* which had run aground during the approach, much to the frustration of her Captain, Thomas Troubridge. By 8 o'clock in the evening, the battle was at its height when Nelson was wounded in the head by a glancing blow from a French shot. He was carried below and at one stage thought himself blinded and dying, but after treatment from the surgeon and some rest, he was able to take the deck again, just in time to see the French flagship, *L'Orient*, glowing brightly in the dark as a savage fire took hold of her. At five past ten she blew up with a violent explosion that temporarily stunned everyone around and brought the battle to a momentary standstill. Despite the loss of their flagship, the French fought on valiantly but by 3am it was obvious that Nelson had won a great victory and the firing slackened off considerably as men on both sides collapsed with exhaustion. Although there was some more firing when daylight came, the battle was almost over and eventually only two French ships-of-the-line and two frigates made good their escape, the rest being either burned or captured. The British had lost around 200 men and had over 700 wounded, but all their ships were afloat. Total French casualties reached over 5,000, including most of the crew of the *L'Orient*.

It was a stunning and total victory, the like of which had never been seen before in naval warfare. As the news spread throughout Europe and eventually reached England, Nelson was showered with well deserved awards including a pension of £2,000 per annum. Officially he was created a Baron, taking the title Baron Nelson of the Nile and Burnham Thorpe, although professional and public opinion thought that he should at least have been made a Viscount. The grateful East India Company, now that the threat to India had been removed, made a grant of £10,000 while the heads of various Mediterranean states, also relieved that the threatening and aggressive French had been defeated fell over themselves to bestow orders, decorations and presents upon him. However, all this took time (it was almost two months before news of the victory officially reached England) and in the immediate aftermath of the battle Nelson suffered a severe reaction to the months of strain, the rigours of the battle and the painful wound to his head. After spending a fortnight at Aboukir Bay organising the repair of his ships and captured enemy vessels, the care of his wounded, the burial of the dead, the general administration of his fleet and dictating various reports and dispatches, he finally set sail in the battered *Vanguard* for the port of Naples. During the voyage he became seriously ill (little wonder!) but after almost a month at sea he had largely recovered by the time the *Vanguard* dropped anchor in the Bay of Naples on 15 September 1798. His life was never to be the same again.

Going ashore to a hero's welcome, Nelson stayed at the Palazzo Sessa, the home of the British Ambassador Sir William Hamilton and his young wife Emma. Emma Hamilton was originally of poor birth but by a combination of good luck and her own calculating determination, she had risen to her present position and was accepted by all at the court of Naples as a woman of position and substance. She immediately took Nelson under her wing, organising parties, dinners and fêtes in his honour and rapidly became inextricably part of his life. Despite Nelson's sense of duty and honour, and his undoubted loyalty to his own wife, he gradually fell under Emma's spell and in time she became his constant companion and mistress. There can be no doubt that the circumstances were much to blame, but Nelson had shown himself in the past to be susceptible to the advances of the fair sex and he was no doubt flattered by the attentions of this attractive woman who in turn was eager to be associated with the hero of the hour. Most historians agree that Nelson, particularly in his later years, was almost unbearably vain and began to think that anything he did would be admired and accepted by the world at large. Although many people close to him, including his loyal captains, tried to warn him of the dangers of the situation, he would take no notice and his relationship with Emma Hamilton has become one of the great scandals of history.

Despite his new entanglements, Nelson was characteristically not idle for long. Even after the defeat inflicted on the French fleet at the Nile and the loss of their expeditionary army in Egypt, the French Army was still the most powerful in Europe and Bonaparte himself made good an escape to France. By the end of the year French forces were advancing down through the Italian peninsula and the Neapolitan army, under the Austrian General Mack, was defeated north of Rome. On 23 December, the *Vanguard* sailed from Naples, together with over 20 other naval and merchant vessels, evacuating the Neapolitan royal family and the rest of their court and senior government officials. The convoy sailed through violent storms to Palermo, Sicily, where the royal family and their followers disembarked to set up court at the Colli Palace. Among those evacuated were the Hamiltons, who sailed with Nelson aboard his flagship. Once in Sicily, Nelson and the Hamiltons shared a grand villa near the harbour where Emma could entertain and indulge in the extravagant social life which so amused her, while Nelson could conduct the administration of his fleet from ashore — only going to sea occasionally when his presence was actually required.

Meanwhile the French were in some difficulties: Russian and Turkish forces captured Corfu, their garrison at Malta was under blockade by Nelson's ships, British were beginning to build up in the Mediterranean while the Austrian army inflicted some significant defeats on the French in the north of Italy. The continued resistance from loyalists in the Papal States and Naples was the last straw and by the spring of 1799 French forces were withdrawing from Naples allowing Nelson to convey the Neapolitan forces back to Naples by mid-June. He now had a fine new flagship, the *Foudroyant* (80 guns), which was under the command of Captain Hardy who was destined to be his flag captain at Trafalgar. Apart from being a large and comfortable ship, the *Foudroyant* also carried what to some appeared a rather macabre piece of furniture. It was a coffin made, at the behest of Captain Ben Hallowell of the *Swiftsure*, from the timbers of the mainmast of the *L'Orient* and presented to Nelson as a gift. He was much taken with this unusual item and had it installed in his great cabin where it provided a source of wonder and conversation to visitors!

On arrival at Naples there was a period of confusion and wrangling as Nelson negotiated for the surrender of the remaining Republican and Jacobin forces. During this time he also took prisoner Commodore Caracciolo, the former head of the Neapolitan navy who had remained in Naples when the royal family had been evacuated and had then taken command of the newly established Republican navy. He was now accused of treason and tried by court martial aboard the *Foudroyant*, although the court was made up of Neapolitan royalist officers. Not unexpectedly, he was found guilty and sentenced to be hanged. Allowing no time for any appeal, Nelson ordered that the sentence be carried out immediately and the unfortunate man was hung from the yardarm of a Sicilian frigate that very evening. There were many other summary executions ashore when the royalist forces eventually occupied the city again and, because of his association with the royal family, Nelson was assumed by some to have at best stood aside and allowed the situation to develop. When news of these events reached England, there was considerable criticism of Nelson's actions and there is no doubt that it damaged his standing in the eyes of some influential politicians.

With Naples safely restored, King Ferdinand showed his gratitude by awarding Nelson the Dukedom of Brontë, a Sicilian estate. This much appealed to Nelson's sense of vanity and he immediately embraced the title although, at the time, it was not the done thing for English peers to make a public display of foreign titles and orders. After experimenting with several variations he eventually settled for the words 'Nelson and Brontë' as his normal signature and this appears on many letters and documents which can be seen today. However, the King showed no great urge to leave Sicily and the whirl of social life and court affairs continued while Nelson further blotted his reputation by disobeying orders from his new C-in-C, Lord Keith, to send some ships to support him off

Minorca. Nelson had decided that Minorca was not in any danger and he preferred to keep his ships where they were, supporting the Neapolitan forces.

At the beginning of 1800, Lord Keith came to Palermo and took Nelson under his orders and together they sailed to intercept a French fleet attempting to run reinforcements to Malta. Leading a small weather squadron, Nelson was ordered ahead and after a long chase overhauled and captured the *Le Généreux*, an 80-gun ship-of-the-line. Despite this success, Nelson's relationship with Keith was strained, and coupled with the fact that Sir William Hamilton had been relieved of his position as ambassador to the Neapolitan court, he requested that he also be relieved so that he could return home. Permission was given but, instead of sailing home in his flagship as he was entitled to do, he decided to travel overland through Europe, accompanying Sir William and Emma Hamilton. This plan was not without its dangers as the French were advancing through Italy again and in fact Nelson's party barely escaped being captured at one point. Reaching Ancona, on the Adriatic coast, they were conveyed aboard a Russian man-of-war to Trieste and then travelled overland to Vienna where they stayed for some weeks. At the end of September the leisurely journey was restarted and the party travelled to Prague and then via the River Elbe to Dresden. Finally Hamburg was reached late in October and after vainly waiting for a British frigate to come for them, the party booked a passage on a mail packet and stepped ashore at Yarmouth on Thursday 6 November, 1800. Nelson had been away from England for almost three years.

His homecoming was not all that he had hoped for. Although the ordinary people turned out in the streets to cheer him, his wife quickly realised the situation between her husband and Emma Hamilton, and by January 1801 she finally left Nelson after an argument and never saw him again. The press and cartoonists had a field day with the strange *ménage à trois* which was Nelson and the Hamiltons, and Nelson himself was snubbed by the King when presented at court. In the circumstances it was as well that Nelson's services were required at sea and he travelled to Plymouth in January 1801 to hoist his flag as Second in Command of the Channel Fleet aboard the *San Josef* (the ship he had captured at the battle of St Vincent), commanded by his old flag captain, Hardy. He was now a Vice-Admiral of the Blue, but on joining the main fleet in its anchorage at Torbay, he was instructed to hoist his flag on the *St George*, another three-decker but one with a shallower draught which would be more suitable for his next assignment which was to be in the Baltic.

While anchored in Torbay, he was enthralled to hear that, at last, he was a father. His mistress, Emma Hamilton, had given birth in secret to a healthy girl, to be named

Horatia. From the tone of his letters, it is obvious that Nelson was overjoyed, and yet saddened and frustrated that he could not advertise the fact to the world at large. Almost up to the time of his death, Nelson and Emma maintained a fiction that they were looking after the child for a seaman serving aboard one of Nelson's ships. It may well be the fact that his own wife never bore him any children, despite living together for almost five years in Norfolk, that formed one of the reasons as to why he allowed himself to become infatuated with Emma Hamilton. Whether this was so or not, the birth of the child certainly set the final seal on the new relationship which was maintained despite public and official disapproval for the rest of Nelson's remaining years.

In the meantime a complex situation had developed in northern waters where the Baltic states of Denmark, Sweden and Russia had allied themselves in what was termed an 'armed neutrality'. With France resurgent on the continent after having defeated Austria, the northern states were anxious not to give any excuse for an attack on their territories and therefore declared that they would not allow their ships to be stopped by British warships enforcing the blockade of continental Europe, while at the same time they attempted to close the Baltic to British trade, seizing several British ships. This situation could not be tolerated as the Royal Navy was extremely reliant on supplies from this region of timber, tar, cordage and other supplies vital for the building and repair of its ships. It was therefore decided to send a powerful fleet to the Baltic to enforce British supremacy and, if necessary, to destroy or neutralise the various opposing fleets.

Nelson sailed from Torbay and joined the rest of the British fleet under Admiral Sir Hyde Parker off Yarmouth in March 1801. Although nominally second-in-command, Nelson succeeded in persuading the cautious Parker to adopt some of his plans. Arriving in the Kattegat at the end of the month, the fleet anchored while Hyde Parker attempted to negotiate with the Danes who steadfastly refused to alter their position. The Commander-in-Chief was reluctant to proceed further but eventually, at Nelson's instigation, the British fleet set sail southwards into the narrow sound between Denmark and Sweden. The actual passage turned out be an anticlimax as the Swedish batteries on the east side remained silent and so the British ships were able to keep to that side of channel, well outside the range of powerful guns in the Danish fort at Kronenborg on the west side but, on reaching Copenhagen, the true extent of the task ahead became apparent. The approach to the harbour and city was protected by the massive Trekroner fort which mounted over 70 heavy guns while the Danish fleet of 18 ships was anchored in a solid line stretching south-east from the fort. These ships were basically floating gun batteries as their masts and yards had been struck down and together they mounted well over 600 guns. The waters off the city were dangerously shoaled and could only be navigated through two channels, the inner of which followed the line of the Danish fleet while the outer, and deeper, channel ran parallel but out of gunshot range.

Nelson's plan was to lead a dozen British ships-of-the-line through to the south end of the sound via the outer channel. These would then approach the Danish fleet from the south-east where they would be furthest away from the dangerous Trekroner fort which would be distracted by the fire from several frigates. In the meantime, Hyde Parker would stand off with the rest of the British fleet at the northern end of the channel where he would be in a position to engage any Russian force which might materialise and could appear to threaten the northern end of the Danish line. Nelson transferred his flag to the *Elephant 74* which was commanded by one of his captains from the Nile, Thomas Foley. This move was necessary as only the smaller 74s and other two-deckers would be able to pass into the shallow waters of the inner channel, another reason why Hyde Parker had to stand off in the deeper water with the larger ships. On 1 April 1801 Nelson set off down the outer channel with his force of ships and moored at the southern end. That evening he was up for most of the night, dictating orders and

Opposite:
Nelson's only child, his daughter Horatia, was born in 1801 — shortly before he sailed for the Baltic. He and Emma Hamilton went to great lengths to conceal the birth and pretended that the father was a seaman aboard one of Nelson's ships. The portrait shows Horatia at the age of two years. *National Maritime Museum*

dining and entertaining some of his captains. Nelson certainly knew how to play his luck for, having wafted down the channel on a favourable northerly wind, the next day a southerly breeze blew up enabling the planned attack to go ahead immediately. Accordingly the ships weighed anchor and the action commenced around half past ten that morning.

At the start, things seemed to be going disastrously wrong. Two 74s, *Bellona* and *Russell*, went aground on shoals and were unable to play any effective part in the battle, while Nelson's old *Agamemnon*, unable to weather the shoals and get into the channel, never came into action. With the main force reduced by a quarter, Nelson's remaining ships were pitched into a fierce and unrelenting action against the well-prepared Danish ships who exchanged shot for shot and showed no signs of slackening. Indeed, as their men were killed or wounded, they were able to ferry out replacements from the shore. After almost three hours Hyde Parker, who was some four miles away and prevented by a foul wind from edging closer to give any support, could see that things were not going well and made a signal ordering Nelson to break off the action. When appraised of this, he showed considerable agitation and after a while he turned to his flag captain and said, 'You know, Foley, I have only one eye. I have the right to be blind sometimes!' At which he raised his telescope to his blind eye and uttered the immortal words, 'I really do not see the signal!'

The action continued but shortly afterwards several Danish ships struck their colours (surrendered) and two of Hyde Parker's ships arrived at the northern end of the line, causing others to strike. In the meantime, Nelson had sent a diplomatically worded note to the Danish commander, the Prince Regent, suggesting that further heavy loss of Danish lives could be avoided if a truce was agreed. As the negotiations continued, a ceasefire was ordered by both sides at around 4 o'clock in the afternoon and this was eventually confirmed as a 24hr truce. The next day, Nelson was plunged into a round of diplomatic negotiations which he considered to be outside his abilities. Nevertheless, after several days intensive bargaining, a 14-week armistice was agreed which, it was

Forestilling af Slaget d. 2den April 1801. om Eftermiddagen Klokken 3, da Admiral Lord Nelson sendte Parlementer Baaden i Land. Krigsskibet 3 Kroner. 2, Krigsskibet Dannemark. 3, Fregatten Iris. 4 Blokskibet Dannebrog, seiler fra Battallien da Ilden var udbrudt, og kort efter sprang Luften. 5 Lord Nelsons Skib. 6, Admiral Parker's Skib. 7, det store Batterie. 8, det lidet Batterie. 9 Parlementer Baaden med tvende Engelske Officerer.

anticipated, would give the British enough time to continue into the Baltic and deal with the Russian fleet. In the event this was not necessary as news came that Czar Paul I had been assassinated and shortly afterwards the new Czar agreed to the release of all impounded British ships and ordered his fleet not to engage in hostilities. As the Swedish fleet remained resolutely at anchor behind the impregnable defences of Karlskrona, there was little outstanding business and Hyde Parker was recalled, leaving Nelson as Commander-in-Chief. It was not until mid-June that Nelson himself was relieved and able to return to England.

The rewards for his actions in Copenhagen were muted and he was made a Viscount, a modest enough accolade when it is realised that successful Admirals were generally rewarded with an Earldom, a rank not achieved by Nelson even after two spectacular victories. Undoubtedly his personal position was one factor, but also the government was anxious to avoid unnecessarily offending the Danes with whom delicate negotiations continued for some time. Typically, Nelson's thoughts were for his men and right up to the time of his death he sought to obtain a wider recognition of their services and to provide more assistance for the wounded and their families. However, once again Nelson was not left idle for long. By this time he was well established as the foremost of Britain's fighting Admirals and his services were immediately required to take command of the naval forces assembled around Britain's south-east coastline to protect the country against an expected French invasion. Although he took part in a few minor actions against invasion forces gathering in places such as Boulogne, he generally found this a frustrating period and was glad when the Peace of Amiens, signed in March 1802, allowed him to stand down and settle at his new home at Merton, in Surrey.

Originally a large farmhouse, the estate at Merton was convenient

Opposite:
An engraving showing the furious fighting at the Battle of Copenhagen. It was on this occasion that Nelson put his telescope to his blind eye and claimed that he could not see any signal ordering him to withdraw.
National Maritime Museum

Above:
A Danish view of the fighting at Copenhagen showing the boat, in the right foreground, carrying Nelson's offer of a truce under a white flag. National Maritime Museum

for reaching London or for travelling by coach down to the naval base at Portsmouth. It had been chosen by Emma Hamilton and the curious arrangement whereby Nelson, Emma and Sir William all lived happily under one roof was continued. After years of active service, Nelson was glad to be in his new home and his letters reveal that this was one of the happiest periods of his life when he was able to enjoy the rewards of his activities. During 1802 he made a well documented tour of the Midlands and South Wales accompanied, as ever, by Emma and Sir William, as well as other members of his household. Whatever his personal situation, he was now known throughout the country as a great leader and a famous hero, and was assured an enthusiastic and cheering reception wherever he went. However, this happy period in his life was all too short and towards its close was marred by the death of Sir William Hamilton with whom, despite the relationship between himself and Emma Hamilton, he had maintained a firm and companionable friendship.

The Peace of Amiens turned out to be short-lived and war with Napoleon's France broke out again in May 1803. Nelson at once took up an appointment as Commander-in-Chief of the Mediterranean fleet and sailed from Portsmouth in his new flagship, the *Victory*, on 20 May 1803. Once on station, his task was the familiar one of blockading the French fleet at Toulon as well as keeping an eye on other potential trouble spots in the Mediterranean and generally assisting and supporting any states friendly to Britain and her cause. After rejecting Malta as a base, he eventually used an anchorage at the northern end of Sardinia. In the meantime the French showed little desire for action and it was not until spring 1804 that they showed signs of stirring, the occasional small force leaving Toulon for exercises when the opportunity offered. In August of that year a new commander was appointed to the French fleet, Admiral Villeneuve, under orders to prepare his ships to take part in an invasion of England. At the end of the year Spain entered the war alongside France, and England was now faced with the terrifying prospect of the two nations' fleets combining in enough strength to brush aside the Royal Navy in the English Channel long enough for a successful invasion to be launched from the ports of France and the Low Countries. Thus, when the frigate *Active* came racing into the Sardinian anchorage on 19 January 1805 flying the signal 'The Enemy is at Sea', there was considerable excitement and apprehension.

In many ways the situation was similar to that which led up to the Battle of the Nile in 1798. Although the French fleet was out, and was known to be carrying a large body of troops, its exact destination was clouded in mystery. Despite the threat to England, it was quite possible that Napoleon had some other objective and every possibility had to be checked out. It was times like this when Nelson was often heard to bemoan the lack of frigates, fast sailing scouts which he could dispatch on information-gathering missions. After much searching involving sailing the length of the Mediterranean it was discovered that the French had returned to Toulon after only a few days because of bad weather. However, they did not stay there for long and at the end of March Villeneuve sailed again, this time bound for Martinique in the West Indies where he was to rendezvous with another force of 20 French ships which would sail from Brest. Once again Nelson was in the dark, but following some slender clues and battling against foul winds, he eventually reached Gibraltar and received confirmation that Villeneuve had already passed by almost a month ahead of him and had been joined by seven Spanish ships from Cadiz.

After reviewing Villeneuve's possible options, Nelson decided that he must be heading for the West Indies and accordingly ordered his fleet to set course in pursuit. This was an extremely brave decision as, had Villeneuve in fact managed to sail towards the Channel and unite with the Brest Fleet, the British forces stationed there under Cornwallis would have been outnumbered and a successful invasion might have occurred. However, as usual, Nelson was right and his experienced ships made a much faster crossing of

Opposite:
Collingwood was a lifelong friend of Nelson's and his second-in-command at Trafalgar. This illustration shows him in the uniform of a Vice-Admiral of the Red. *Author's Collection*

Painted by H. Howard, R.A.

Engraved by W. Holl.

CUTHBERT, LORD COLLINGWOOD.

VICE ADMIRAL OF THE RED.

Presented to Greenwich Hospital by his Family.

FISHER, SON & C?. LONDON & PARIS.

the Atlantic than had the French, making up 10 days of lost time. On reaching Barbados, Nelson obtained his first positive confirmation that Villeneuve was in the West Indies but incorrect intelligence then led him off on a wild goose chase southwards towards Trinidad. The French Admiral, on hearing that Nelson was close behind him, panicked and abandoned his troops on various French islands before setting sail back across the Atlantic. Again, without the full facts being available to him, Nelson correctly deduced the French intentions and immediately set off in pursuit. Ahead of him he sent the brig *Curieux* with news of his actions and intentions and by good fortune this fast sailing ship fell in with the French and was able to obtain an accurate assessment of their strength, speed and course, before racing on to England where her commander rushed to London to appraise Lord Barham, the First Lord of the Admiralty, of this vital intelligence. Barham was an exceedingly active and efficient man (although he was 79) and immediately issued orders which enabled Admiral Calder to be off Finisterre on 22 July 1805 in time to intercept Villeneuve's returning ships. Given the difficulties of communications in those days, this was little short of a miraculous achievement and yet it was squandered by Calder who fought an adequate but disappointing action over several days which allowed Villeneuve and the majority of his ships to escape to the safety of Vigo Bay and thence to Ferrol.

In the meantime Nelson had arrived at Gibraltar two days before Calder's action to find that, at that moment, there was no news of Villeneuve. Briefly setting foot on shore, for the first time in over two years, he quickly replenished his ships and set off northwards to join up with Cornwallis off Brest. Here he learnt that the combined French and Spanish fleets were safely in harbour and so continued on to England where he arrived on 18 August 1805. His time on shore was brief as the combined enemy fleets posed a massive threat and the whole nation saw Nelson as the man to fight and defeat them. After less than four weeks ashore, he was again at Portsmouth preparing to board the *Victory* for his final battle. As he walked to the quayside there were amazing scenes as hundreds of people crowded to see him leave. Everybody expected a battle and from his remarks and writings, it seems clear that Nelson himself thought it unlikely that he would ever see his mistress, daughter, home or country again.

By the end of September he had rejoined the rest of the fleet off Cadiz where Villeneuve and the combined fleets were now in harbour. The French Admiral was in an impossible dilemma for he knew if he came out a battle was unavoidable, and it was one which he would probably lose. On the other hand, he knew that his replacement, Admiral Rosily, was already on his way from Paris and that he would have to return home to face probable death or imprisonment at the hands of Napoleon for failing to complete the emperor's grand but impractical plans for the invasion of England. Feeling, perhaps, that he might as well be hung for a sheep as a lamb, he gave the order to sail and the combined fleet of 33 ships-of-the-line began to leave Cadiz on the morning of 19 October 1805. British frigates immediately spotted this foray and the information was relayed to Nelson who was standing offshore below the horizon. He was in no hurry to force the action, waiting until all the enemy ships were at sea and far enough from Cadiz so that they could not easily return there if threatened. Thus it was not until the morning of the 21st that the opposing fleets drew close, Nelson having altered course during the night to bring about the desired junction off Cape Trafalgar, some 40 miles south of Cadiz.

There were 33 enemy ships-of-the-line against Nelson's 27, although both sides had a number of frigates as well. The Combined fleet was in something of a muddle as it was heading south and attempting to change from its cruising formation of five columns into a single line of battle. As soon as Villeneuve realised a battle was unavoidable he ordered his ships to wear and head back towards Cadiz, sailing on the port tack in the light westerly breeze. The result of all this manoeuvring left the ships in a crescent shaped line, concave to the British fleet approaching in two columns from the south-west. Nelson had given a considerable amount of thought to problems involved in fighting a

successful fleet action at sea, and had discussed ideas and tactics with his captains while patrolling off Cadiz. His original plan called for three columns to break the enemy line at separate points and bring about localised superiority of force, but on sighting the enemy he realised that his cruising disposition of two columns consisting of 13 ships led by his second-in-command, Collingwood, aboard the *Royal Sovereign* and the remaining 14 led by himself and the *Victory* would achieve the desired effect. Due to the light winds, the rate of closing was slow and there was plenty of time for all the necessary preparations for action and for any instructions to be signalled. While this was going on Nelson retired to his cabin to write a last letter. Addressed to no one in particular, it was an open document expressing his hope that Emma Hamilton and his 'adopted' daughter, Horatia, would be cared for in the event of his death, and he asked Captains Hardy and Blackwood to witness it. A little later he returned again to his cabin, now stripped for action and composed his last writing — a prayer which has become famous and is repeated below:

'May the Great God, whom I worship, grant to my Country, and for the benefit of Europe in general, a great and glorious Victory; and may no misconduct in anyone tarnish it; and may humanity after Victory be the predominant feature in the British Fleet. For myself, individually, I commit my life to him who made me, and may his blessing light upon my endeavours for serving my Country faithfully. To him I resign myself and the just cause which is entrusted to me to defend. Amen. Amen. Amen.'

Back on deck he found there was still some three miles between the fleets and he ordered bands to play so that the seamen might be entertained. He then ordered his famous signal to be flown, 'England expects that every man will do his duty', and this was received with cheers aboard the British ships. Despite Nelson's efforts to catch up with the enemy, it was Collingwood, aboard the

Above:
Nelson falls mortally wounded on the quarterdeck of the *Victory* as the battle rages around him. A famous painting by Denis Dighton which can be seen at the National Maritime Museum. *National Maritime Museum*

fast-sailing *Royal Sovereign*, who made the first contact just before midday as he passed through the mid-point of the enemy line between the 112-gun *Santa Ana* and the *Fougueux*, a French 74. As the rest of Collingwood's column came up they engaged the remaining ships in the rear half of the enemy line.

In the meantime, the *Victory* came under heavy fire from several ships as she approached the leading group of the enemy and by the time she passed through the enemy line at about half past twelve she was already badly damaged. With her steering almost shot away, Captain Hardy managed to round up and lay alongside the *Redoubtable*, a French 74 ably commanded by Captain Jean Lucas. Shortly after, the British *Téméraire* came up on the *Redoubtable*'s disengaged side and she, in turn, was then set upon by the *Fougueux* so that no less than four ships were locked together, exchanging blow for blow as they swung slowly in the wind. Among Captain Lucas' preparations for battle had been the positioning of marksmen in the crosstrees and these kept up a steady fire on the deck of the *Victory*, only some fifty feet below. At around 1.35pm Nelson was on the quarterdeck, pacing up and down with Hardy when he fell to the deck, hit in the right shoulder by a musket ball fired by one of *Redoubtable*'s marksmen. The plunging shot had caused massive internal injuries and had broken Nelson's spine. As Hardy rushed up to him, he smiled grimly and said, 'They have done for me at last'.

Above:
A contemporary engraving of the Death of Nelson after the famous painting by Arthur Devis.
Author's Collection

Opposite:
The plaque on the deck of HMS *Victory* showing the spot where Nelson fell mortally wounded at the Battle of Trafalgar.
ASM

There was no lack of willing hands to carry the stricken Admiral down to the cockpit, already full of wounded men. The surgeon, Mr Beatty, quickly confirmed the dying man's own diagnosis and saw that there was little he could do except try and make the great man's last moments as comfortable as possible. Hardy returned to the deck where he was needed as the battle neared its crisis but eventually, at around three, he was able to come below and report that victory was assured with some twelve or fourteen enemy ships already taken. In the next hour, as Nelson's life slowly slipped away, he fretted over the conduct of the battle but was eventually reassured when Hardy came below again to report more ships captured.

Nelson now entreated Hardy to take care of Lady Hamilton and, seeking comfort from his stalwart and long-standing flag captain, whispered, 'Kiss me, Hardy'. After this, and knowing that a great victory had been won, he said, 'Now I am satisfied; Thank God I have done my duty'. After that he lay exhausted, speaking occasionally only with great difficulty and at around half past four, three hours after being hit and as the sounds of battle began to fade away, he died.

Within the British fleet there was a welter of conflicting emotions. A great victory had been won but the cost had been terrible. As well as the loss of their greatly loved and respected Admiral, there were over 1,500 British casualties including 454 dead and many of the ships were barely in a fit state to sail. In the Combined fleet the carnage had been terrible with almost 3,000 dead and many more wounded. In the aftermath of the battle a fierce gale blew up and many of the captured ships were blown ashore and wrecked. The battered *Victory* was towed to Gibraltar for repairs while Nelson's body was undressed

and preserved by the surgeon in a cask of spirits. With a jury rig set, *Victory* sailed for England and arrived at Spithead on 5 December.

In the meantime news of the great battle at Trafalgar reached London on 5 November 1805 and while rejoicing in the victory, the nation was plunged into mourning for its brave Admiral. Newspapers and broadsheets printed graphic and detailed accounts of the battle and the rewards for the survivors fell thick and fast in the form of peerages, knighthoods, promotions and medals. Strangely, Nelson's family was rewarded by the granting of an Earldom to his brother, the Reverend William Nelson and subsequently a grand mansion, Trafalgar House, was erected near Salisbury for him to live in. Given the relative meanness of the awards to Nelson in his own lifetime, one cannot but wonder at the attitudes which resulted in such an irony. However, whatever the government's ambivalence to Nelson while he was alive, they did him proud after his death. Despite Nelson's own wish to be buried at Burnham Thorpe in Norfolk, it was decided that he would be interred, with great ceremony, at St Paul's Cathedral. The funeral ceremony was perhaps the grandest and most complex ever arranged for any Englishman, even considering the later formal state funerals of monarchs and Churchill.

Nelson's body lay in state in the Painted Hall at the Greenwich Naval Hospital before being taken, early on the morning of 9 January 1806, in a ceremonial barge some four miles upriver to the steps below Whitehall accompanied by a massive flotilla of official craft. His coffin was conveyed to the Admiralty where it lay awaiting the start of a formal procession to St Paul's, to be conveyed on a specially constructed funeral car which was intended to represent his flagship with the figure of Fame bearing a laurel wreath on the prow and the inscription '*HMS Victory*' on the stern section. The actual procession was so long that the Scots Greys, heading the column, are reported to have reached St Paul's before the parties of Army and Navy officers had left the Admiralty. It was two o'clock before the funeral car reached the steps of Wren's great masterpiece

Top:
The river funeral procession from Greenwich to Whitehall Steps passes under London Bridge. A contemporary aquatint. *Author's Collection*

Above
St Paul's Cathedral, London. The last resting place of Vice Admiral Lord Nelson. *ASM*

Opposite:
An engraving which captures the solemn dignity of Nelson's interment at St Paul's Cathedral. *National Maritime Museum*

ERECTED AT THE PUBLIC EXPENSE
TO THE MEMORY OF
VICE-ADMIRAL HORATIO, VISCOUNT NELSON, K.B.
TO RECORD HIS SPLENDID AND UNPARALLELLED ACHIEVEMENTS,
DURING A LIFE SPENT IN THE SERVICE OF HIS COUNTRY,
AND TERMINATED IN THE MOMENT OF VICTORY BY A GLORIOUS DEATH,
IN THE MEMORABLE ACTION OFF CAPE TRAFALGAR ON THE XXI OF OCTOBER MDCCCV.
LORD NELSON WAS BORN ON THE XXIX OF SEPTEMBER MDCCLVIII.
THE BATTLE OF THE NILE WAS FOUGHT ON THE I OF AUGUST MDCCXCVIII,
THE BATTLE OF COPENHAGEN ON THE II OF APRIL, MDCCCI.

and was carried into the cathedral by a party of 12 men from the *Victory* under a canopy borne by six admirals. During the service, the coffin lay in the centre of a circular arena, beneath the great dome, and was lowered into the crypt at the end. As it disappeared, a large party of men from the *Victory* fell upon the ship's tattered battle ensigns, which had been intended to drape the coffin, and each tore himself a small part of the flag as a personal memorial to the man who had commanded and fought with them, and had made the final and ultimate sacrifice for the country which he loved so much.

What of his family and friends? Emma Hamilton was spurned by officialdom and eventually died in poverty across the Channel, at Calais, in January 1815. Nelson's daughter, Horatia, lived to a ripe old age but was not made aware of her illustrious parentage until quite late in life. Several of her descendants are alive today. Lady Frances Nelson, his estranged wife, was granted a pension of £2,000 a year and lived out her remaining years in Exmouth, South Devon. The Earldom granted to Nelson's brother, William, has been passed on and is currently held by the eighth Earl Nelson so that, almost 200 years after his death, the name of Nelson is still alive to remind everyone of the stirring deeds and selfless sacrifice which will forever be associated with him.

Above:
Nelson's flag captain, Thomas Masterman Hardy, shown as Vice-Admiral in 1834. A portrait, also on view at the National Maritime Museum, by Richard Evans.
National Maritime Museum

Left:
The magnificent memorial to Nelson which stands in the south side of the transept at St Paul's Cathedral. The tomb itself is in the crypt below the cathedral and takes pride of place among the tombs of many other distinguished soldiers, sailors and airmen. *ASM*

Britannia Triumphant

THE MOST DECISIVE and GLORIOUS
NAVAL VICTORY
that has ever been obtained

THE Victorious BRITISH FLEET
Commanded by the most RENOWNED, most GALLANT, and ever to be LAMENTED HERO,

Admiral Lord Viscount
NELSON

The defeated combined Enemy Fleets of FRANCE & SPAIN Commanded by **Admirals Villeneuve and Gravina**

This memorable Action was Fought off Cape TRAFALGAR near the Entrance of the Straits of **GIBRALTAR** *on the 21st October last* **1805**

THE ENGLISH FLEET consisted of ~
27 SHIPS OF THE LINE

	GUNS	MEN
VICTORY (Adm. Lord Visc. Nelson)	110	837
ROYAL SOVEREIGN (V. Adm. Collingwood)	110	837
BRITANNIA	100	800
TEMERAIRE	98	738
PRINCE	98	738
TONNANT	84	650
BELLEISLE	74	590
REVENGE	74	590
MARS	74	590
NEPTUNE	98	738
DEFIANCE	74	590
CONQUERER	74	..
DEFENCE	74	..
COLOSSUS	74	..
LEVIATHAN	74	..
ACHILLE	74	..
BELLEROPHON	74	..
MINOTAUR	74	..
ORION	74	..
SWIFTSURE	74	..
POLYPHEMUS	64	500
AFRICA	64	500
AGAMEMNON	64	500
DREADNOUGHT	98	738
AJAX	80	650
THUNDERER	74	590

Total 2,178 17,076

The Combined Enemy Fleet superior in Guns 474 in Men 8,124

THE Combined FLEETS OF FRANCE & SPAIN ~
33 SHIPS OF THE LINE

		GUNS	MEN	
SANTISIMA TRINIDAD	(s)	140	1200	Taken and Destroyed
BUCENTAURE	(f)	84	800	Taken and Destroyed
RAYO	(s)	100	1000	Taken and Destroyed
PRINCIPE de ASTURIAS	(s)	112	1100	Escaped
INDOMPTABLE	(f)	84	800	Destroyed
FOUGUEUX	(f)	74	700	Taken and Destroyed
ACHILLE	(f)	74	700	Blown-up
SANTA ANA	(s)	112	1100	Taken, but got away
MONTANES	(s)	74	700	Escaped
HEROS	(f)	74	700	Escaped
SAN LEANDRO	(s)	64	600	Dismasted, but Escaped
SAN JUSTO	(s)	74	700	Dismasted, but Escaped
SAN ILDEFONSO	(s)	74	700	Taken
LE SWIFTSURE	(f)	74	700	Taken, formerly English
ALGÉSIRAS	(f)	74	700	Escaped, much damaged
PLUTON	(f)	74	700	Escaped
NEPTUNE	(f)	84	800	Escaped
BAHAMA	(s)	74	700	Taken
SAN NEPOMUCENO	(s)	74	700	Taken
MONARCA	(s)	74	700	Destroyed
SAN FRANCISCO de ASIS	(s)	74	700	Destroyed
ARGONAUTE	(f)	74	700	On Shore at Cadiz
LE BERWICK	(f)	74	700	Escaped, formerly English
L'AIGLE	(f)	74	700	Taken and Destroyed
INTRÉPIDE	(f)	74	700	Taken and Burnt
SAN AGUSTIN	(s)	74	700	Taken and Burnt
REDOUTABLE	(f)	74	700	Taken and Destroyed
ARGONAUTA	(f)	80	800	Escaped
FORMIDABLE	(f)	80	800	Escaped
MONT-BLANC	(f)	74	700	Escaped but later Captured
SCIPION	(f)	74	700	Escaped
DUGUAY-TROUIN	(f)	74	700	Escaped
NEPTUNO	(s)	84	800	Destroyed

(f) Denotes French Ships
(s) Denotes Spanish Ships

Total 2,652 25,200

Four ADMIRALS taken, One killed, and Three wounded.

Above:
Copy of a contemporary poster announcing the outcome of the Battle of Trafalgar and listing the names and details of all participating ships. Such posters were a common means of distributing important news before the days of radio and TV.

2: NELSON WAS
HERE

Nelson was a fighting seaman and consequently most of the events which made him famous occurred at sea and, with the notable exception of HMS *Victory*, the ships in which he sailed have long since disappeared. It is, of course, not possible for most readers to go to sea in a sailing ship and trace his voyages to most corners of the globe but, on land, the story is different and it is possible in many instances to follow Nelson's life by visiting the places with which he is directly associated. Obviously most of these are in Britain and are duly described, but there are many interesting places to be visited abroad where a distinct Nelson connection can be found and these are also described, although generally not in such great detail.

So, let's start at the beginning! Nelson was born at Burnham Thorpe, a quiet and isolated rural community near the north Norfolk coast. Today it can be reached by taking the A148 road from King's Lynn towards Cromer. After only a few miles a turn off to the left leads on to the B1153 which can be followed over the fertile undulating countryside to the small village of Burnham Market, a crossroads at the centre of no less than seven different Burnhams, of which Burnham Thorpe can be reached by taking a well-signposted lane for a couple of miles to the south-east. Coming over the brow of a hill, almost the first building to be seen is the church of All Saints' which stands at the northern end of the village. It was here that Nelson's father, the Reverend Edmund Nelson was rector, but the rectory itself was at the other end of the village and can be found by following signs to 'Nelson's Birthplace'. The original rectory stood just back from the banks of the River Burn, here a pleasant clear flowing brook only a few feet across. Although the original rectory was demolished after his father's death in 1802, the site is clearly marked by a signpost, and by a plaque set in the wall alongside the lane. Looking over the wall, the handsome building standing well back from the road was built as a replacement for the original rectory and today is a private house as the current rector is responsible for several parishes and lives in Burnham Market.

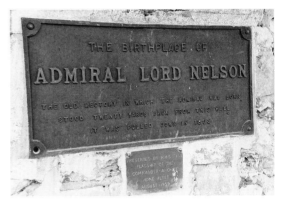

Apart from a modest expansion and many new houses, the character of Burnham Thorpe has probably changed little since Nelson lived and played here as a boy. The river runs through the centre of the village, and the three-quarters of a mile walk to the church where his father ministered is a pleasant stroll through quiet lanes and fields. In the centre, near a bridge over the river, is a painted sign similar to those displayed in other Norfolk villages although this one states with pride that Nelson was born and raised here. As a boy with a running stream outside his front door, it was almost inevitable that his games would include water activities such as the floating of small boats made from twigs and bits of timber. It is easy to imagine a young lad following the course of the river for only a couple of miles until he came to the tidal estuary at Overy Staithe where he would have caught his first glimpse of the sea which was to be his destiny. No doubt he talked local fisherman into taking him out with them and he would have gained an appreciation of the effect of winds and tides on their small craft. Like many other hamlets in this part of Norfolk, time seems to have stood still at the Staithe and the waterfront is overlooked by many buildings that Nelson would still recognise today. A footpath follows the tidal estuary out to Gun Hill, overlooking the sand dunes at the sea's edge and this was a favourite walk of Nelson's in later years. At the top of the village is a pub, the 'Hero', which commemorates his memory.

To return to Burnham Thorpe, the village is, of course, more than just the place where he was born. Apart from his childhood, he spent five long years here with his wife before being called back to sea in 1793 and there are many tangible reminders of both these periods. Although the old rectory is gone, there is a large ornamental pond at the southern end of the grounds and this was created by Nelson, together with his gardener, during his years of enforced idleness. It is generally held that the dimensions of the pond were intended to match the length and beam of a typical sailing man-of-war of the period, roughly 200ft by 50ft, and that Nelson intended to sail model ships upon it. This is quite possibly true as the shape of the pond certainly fits such a description.

In the centre of the village, as would be expected, is the village inn. Today, inevitably, it is known as 'The Lord Nelson' but it was originally 'The Plough' and was already well established when Nelson was born, having been built in 1650. In fact there is a story that he was actually born in the barn which forms an outbuilding to the pub, but this seems highly unlikely and it is more probable that his mother was at home in the rectory when she gave birth on 29 September 1758. However, a visit to the inn is absolutely essential as a step inside is to pass right back to Nelson's time. The inn must be almost unique in having no bar! Instead there is a parlour with wooden tables and benches and, usually, a roaring log fire. To order a drink, one calls the landlord who then disappears into a back room where the beer is drawn directly from taps set in the wooden barrels arranged along the wall. Although almost unheard of today, this style of inn was typical of Nelson's time, and indeed it is recorded that he held a party here for his friends and relatives to celebrate his appointment to command of the *Agamemnon* and his return to sea in 1793. The walls of the room are now hung with prints and illustrations of Nelson and his battles and, while most of them are not contemporary, they provide a suitable backdrop. One should not leave the Lord Nelson without buying a bottle of 'Nelson's Blood' — a rum whose name is derived from the fact that Nelson's body was preserved after Trafalgar in a cask of brandy and wine spirits, the contents of which were later reputed to have been drunk by the crew of the *Victory!*

By far the most significant building in the village is the 600-year old church of All Saints which stands almost alone, surrounded by open fields and a small copse of trees. Nelson's father came here as rector in 1755 with his young wife, Catherine, and both parents are now buried here under the floor of the chancel while outside will be found the graves of his brother Maurice and sister Susannah. There is a fine memorial to Nelson himself, incorporating a lifelike

Above opposite:
Where it all started. Nelson's birthplace is well signposted. *ASM*

Opposite:
This commemorative plaque is set in the wall of the Old Rectory grounds. *ASM*

Above:
Overy Staithe, near Burnham Thorpe, where the tidal estuary leads out to the sea. Nelson often came here as a boy. *ASM*

Previous page:
A statue of Nelson stands in the grounds of Norwich Cathedral, near to the school which he attended in 1767. *ASM*

Above:
The ornamental pond in the rectory grounds is reputed to have been created by Nelson during his period ashore on half pay. The building in the background replaced the original rectory which was demolished in 1802. *ASM*

Right:
All Saints' church at Burnham Thorpe where Nelson's father was rector. *ASM*

Opposite top:
A memorial to the Reverend Edmund Nelson set on the wall of All Saints' church. *ASM*

Opposite far right:
The interior of the 'Lord Nelson' inn at Burnham Thorpe has changed little since Nelson's time and he probably often sat at the fireplace shown in the photo. *ASM*

Opposite below:
The village of Burnham Thorpe is proud of its Nelson connection, as evidenced by this sign. *ASM*

bust, on the chancel wall and beside this are further memorials to his parents. No doubt Nelson would have regularly attended services here, and today there are many reminders of his association with the church and village. At the back of the church are copies of two important documents, the first being the certificate of Nelson's baptism. Born on 29 September, it is recorded that he was baptised at a private ceremony on 6 October, to be followed by a public occasion for friends and family on 15 November, these christenings being carried out in the Purbeck marble bowl of the font still standing near the rear of the church. The other document is a copy of the entries in the church register in relation to a wedding where one of the witnesses is Horatio Nelson who would then have been almost 11 years old. It is fascinating to note that he signs himself as 'Horace', although this has been corrected to 'Horatio' by his father. Apparently the young Nelson preferred the appellation Horace and it was used informally in the family until he grew up.

There are a number of relics from HMS *Victory* here also, the main one being a large wooden cross mounted on the rood beam across the chancel arch. This is actually made from the gallant ship's timbers, as is the wooden lectern below. On the wall at the entrance to the base of the bell tower is a wood and copper tablet commemorating the restoration of the church bell in September 1958. The materials in this plaque again come from HMS *Victory*.

After the end of World War 2, the mighty battleship HMS *Nelson* was laid up and scrapped. However, one of the ship's crests, cast in bronze and presented in 1955 to mark the 150th anniversary of Trafalgar, is preserved here in the church along with two of the ship's ensigns which hang in the west corners of the aisle. Although not having any Nelson connection there are also two other more tattered ensigns which came from the battlecruiser *Indomitable* and were flown by that ship at the Battle of Jutland in 1916. Stowed amongst the neat lines of pews are some beautifully embroidered kneelers showing variously HMS *Victory* and the crest of HMS *Nelson*. Finally, along the south wall are a series of

display boards giving an illustrated and interesting account of the life of Nelson. Set amongst these, mounted on the wall, is a framed copy of Nelson's last prayer, while at the back of the nave are facsimile copies of the issues of the *London Gazette* and *Times* describing the Battle of Trafalgar and also Nelson 's funeral and interment at St Paul's.

The church itself was in a poor state of repair during Nelson's times for then, as ever, funds for the upkeep and repair of such a large building were hard to come by. By the end of the 19th century it was in a parlous state but fortunately some public funds were made available so that it might be restored in time for the centenary of Trafalgar in 1905. Today the church is a haven of peace and quiet, and a place to reflect on the influences and upbringing which gave Nelson such a strong sense of duty, patriotism and self sacrifice. Some of those influences would also have come from the schools which he attended and there are at least two of these, the first of which was the Norwich Grammar school. This was an old established seat of learning which still stands, set in the grounds of the cathedral, and nearby a statue of Nelson has been erected. He attended the grammar school for approximately one year from late 1767 before completing the rest of his education at Paston School in North Walsham in a period of just over two years from September 1768 until he left to join the Navy. In view of the distance from Burnham Thorpe, he attended both schools as a boarder in company with his brother, William. At the time this red brick building at Paston was fairly new and it stands in all its glory today with a plaque proclaiming that 'Here Nelson Learned His Lessons!'. The school is most proud of its connection with Nelson and can point out to interested visitors the very classroom, still in use, where the young lad studied together with a brick bearing the carved initials HN and a pencil box believed to have belonged to

him. There is also a considerable display of prints, pictures and other items with a Nelson connection. The school is, of course, private property, and the Headmaster should be approached for permission to visit the campus.

There are a number of other houses and places which Nelson would have visited, particularly when he was living at Burnham on half pay between 1788 and 1793. The nearest is the magnificent Holkham Hall and its extensive estate only a couple of miles to the east of Burnham Thorpe, built in the middle of the 18th century for Thomas Coke, the Earl of Leicester, to whom Nelson was obliged to report at intervals to have his forms and declarations signed and witnessed so that he could claim his half-pay pension. This business was conducted in the Earl's study although this is now used as a dining room. Holkham Hall is open to the public throughout the summer months and offers a fascinating insight into 18th century life.

Nelson's youngest sister Catherine married a successful property owner called George Matcham. They lived in some comfort at Barton Hall in the village of Barton Turf near Wroxham on the edge of the Norfolk Broads. Nelson and his wife occasionally visited and stayed with the Matchams and he became very friendly with his brother-in-law. Many years later George Matcham was one of the last people in England to speak with Nelson before he departed for Trafalgar and at that meeting was entrusted with the care of his daughter, Horatia. After Emma Hamilton's death in 1815, Matcham brought the young girl back to Norfolk where she settled and eventually married. Barton Hall still stands, although not open to the public.

Nelson was distantly related, through his mother's family, to Lord Walpole (Sir Hugh Walpole was Britain's first modern prime minister, from 1721 to 1742) who lived in aristocratic splendour at Wolterton Hall, a few miles south of Cromer. Nelson and his wife got into the habit of spending a few weeks each year with the Walpoles as house guests, generally around the Christmas period, while he was on half pay at Burnham. The hall is still the residency of the Walpole family and a continuing programme of restoration and refurbishment of the house and estate has been carried out in recent years.

Some 20 miles south-east of King's Lynn is the small village of Hilborough where Nelson's father had been rector for several years before going to Burnham Thorpe in 1755. He was succeeded by the Reverend Robert Rolfe who was an uncle of Nelson's and the young boy would often visit the rectory for short holidays. In 1785 the living was taken over by Nelson's elder brother, William, resulting in further visits during the period 1788-1793. The 14th century church, another All Saints', contains several memorials to various members of the Nelson family including two brothers who preceded him but died in infancy and are buried next to the altar. It is fascinating to find that this quiet, out of the way, village has connections with the two great commanders of the Napoleonic wars for, apart from Nelson, the Duke of Wellington lived for a while in Hilborough Hall which adjoins the churchyard, although it is not recorded that the two men ever met here.

Just north of Hilborough, on the main A47 road linking King's Lynn to Norwich, stands the old village of Swaffham. Nelson's wife, Fanny, found the bleak winds off the North sea at Burnham a

Opposite top:
The cross above the chancel at All Saints' is made of timber taken from HMS *Victory. ASM*

Opposite:
Paston school at North Walsham where Nelson attended for two years from 1768. The original school is on the left, the other building having been erected in the 1920s. *ASM*

Above:
A plaque on the wall of Paston School. *ASM*

severe trial in winter, and made arrangements to stay in lodgings at Swaffham for various times when Nelson was later away at sea. After her estrangement from Nelson she moved away from Norfolk altogether, but when Nelson finally fathered a child with Emma Hamilton, it was to Swaffham that the young girl was brought to be baptised as Horatia Nelson Thompson, supporting the fiction that the child was not theirs. Emma Hamilton herself was recorded as being the godmother although few people were fooled by this charade. Today, the building which is now Strattons Hotel was originally 'The Villa' in Ash Grove, the home of the Yonge family with whom Nelson was distantly connected and where Emma Hamilton stayed when she visited Norfolk after Nelson's death.

Not far from Burnham Thorpe, a few miles along the coast to the east, is the small port of Wells-next-the-Sea. Nelson is known to have visited here on many occasions and Fanny also rented a house at Buttlands for a while when Nelson was away. This house is now known as Clarence House, a title bestowed on it by Fanny in recognition of her husband's friendship with the Duke of Clarence. Nelson himself struck up a friendship with a lad called Ben Hallowell, the son of a Wells Customs Officer. This was to be a lasting relationship as Ben also joined the Navy and served alongside Nelson on several occasions, notably at the Battle of the Nile. The 'Crown Hotel' at Buttlands, Wells, is reputed to have been frequented by Nelson and it certainly contains many prints and illustrations of his life and battles. Finally, Nelson's sister Susannah married a Wells businessman, Thomas Bolton, and they lived here during their early married life, being visited by Nelson while briefly ashore in 1781.

When Nelson finally sailed away aboard the *Agamemnon* in 1793, he was to destined to see very little of his beloved Norfolk in his remaining 12 years. He was away for

almost four years and when he returned he was no longer an unknown captain but a national hero, a Rear-Admiral and a Knight of the Bath. He was also blind in one eye and suffering from the painful after effects of the loss of his right arm at Tenerife in July 1797. When he came ashore at Portsmouth in early December, it was not to Norfolk that he travelled, but to the spa resort of Bath where Fanny and his father had taken lodgings at 17 New King Street, still standing today. Bath was not unknown to Nelson as it had been popular with his father who often stayed there to take the waters, and he himself had taken lodgings for several months at 2 Pierrepoint Street, near

North Parade, when he had returned from Jamaica in ill health at the end of 1780. This house still stands among the terraces at North Parade, near the town centre, which are popular even today. At the time, Nelson was much taken with Bath and enjoyed walking its broad streets and open parks. He was in good company as it was a popular spot for convalescing officers and its mild climate drew many of his friends from the West Indies when they returned to England. Bath takes its name from the ancient Roman baths, built to take advantage of the mineral-rich waters welling up from springs around the town. These, together with the later Pump Room and Assembly Rooms would all have been known and visited by Nelson during his stay and they are all substantially unchanged from that time. Apart from the horrendous blight of modern motor traffic, central Bath is probably less changed than any other town which Nelson might revisit were he alive today. Nelson left Bath, much restored in health, in April 1781 and travelled to Norfolk where he stayed for a short period with family and friends, but by August he was at sea again and did not return for two years.

His stay at Bath in 1797 following the loss of his arm was brief, and after a few weeks he travelled with his wife up to London where they rented accommodation at 141 Bond Street and it was here that Nelson stayed until his arm was fully healed. Again London, and Bond Street in particular, was not unfamiliar to him. He had first lived here when he returned as a married man from the West Indies at the end of 1787, the start of his long period on half pay. Initially the couple had stayed with his wife's family, the Herberts, at 5 Cavendish Square, just off Oxford Street. This quiet square with its neatly kept gardens is still bordered on two sides by houses from Nelson's time although more modern structures complete the scene. Despite the Nelson connection, No 5 bears a blue plaque giving only details of the later history of the house when it was owned by Quintin Hogg at the turn of the century. Nelson would probably be shocked to find that today part of the building is used as offices by a Spanish trade delegation!

The Nelson's did not stay with their in-laws for long, finding lodgings of their own at 10 Great Marlborough Street and also at 6 Princes Street, both only a few minutes' walk away, off nearby Regent Street. Developments since Nelson's time have removed all traces of the buildings in which he actually stayed and, in any case, it was not long before it became apparent that he was unlikely to be employed for some time and he moved back to the rectory at Burnham Thorpe. However, his Bond Street addresses have survived the test of time and No 141, now renumbered No 147, is occupied by a firm of fine art dealers. The lodgings in Bond Street were convenient for his regular visits to the Admiralty, being only a few minutes' stroll through Piccadilly and St James's. His contacts paid off and he was soon appointed to a new ship with orders to lead a British force into the Mediterranean. Before sailing, he briefly visited his father and returned to a new set of lodgings in Bond Street, this time at No 96. Since that time, the buildings in Bond Street, including what is now New Bond Street, have been renumbered and it is at No 93 that a plaque can be found commemorating Nelson's brief stay. After he left, his wife Fanny repaired to Bath where she found the climate and the company more congenial.

Nelson's subsequent connections with London relate to the period after he returned to England with Emma Hamilton in 1800. The party initially came ashore at Yarmouth on 6 November where

Opposite top:
No 5 Cavendish Square, home of the Herbert family, where Nelson and his new wife stayed when they first returned from the West Indies in 1787. *ASM*

Opposite centre:
No 141 Bond Street was where Nelson came to recover from the loss of his arm at Tenerife. Today this building is now renumbered 147, but a small plaque above the first floor window records the connection. *ASM*

Opposite below:
An aquatint by Thomas Malton showing Cavendish Square in 1800 which gives a good indication of how fashionable parts of London appeared in Nelson's time. *ASM*

Above left:
When Nelson landed in England in 1800 after his overland journey from Naples, he stayed at the 'Wrestler's Inn', Great Yarmouth. Although much altered, this still stands today but is renamed 'Hardy's'. *ASM*

they put up for the night at the 'Wrestler's Inn' near the town centre. This was a typical hostelry of the period and part of it still stands today although it has been altered beyond recognition and renamed 'Hardy's', perhaps in an attempt to draw the Nelson connection. The next day they set off again, initially heading for Roundwood, near Ipswich. This was Nelson's own house which he and Fanny had begun negotiations to purchase just before he sailed for the Mediterranean in 1798. Neither his wife nor father was at home and he continued towards London. Thus he never spent a night in this house and it was sold off shortly afterwards, no trace remaining today as it was demolished in 1960.

Arriving in London, Nelson and the Hamiltons stayed initially at an hotel in King Street, St James's, but after a while he moved to lodgings at 17 Dover Street, not so far from Bond Street, while the Hamilton's took over the house of a friend at 22 Grosvenor Square. By early 1801, Nelson and his wife had split up irreconcilably and he arranged for her to take over the house at Dover Street when he sailed for the Baltic. Eventually the Hamiltons bought a house at 23 Piccadilly and Nelson often stayed and conducted business here when he was in town until after Sir William's death in 1803 when he used lodgings at 19 Piccadilly for the same purpose. Although the streets survive today, the actual houses have been overtaken by subsequent development.

However, Nelson's largest and final home was a substantial house at Merton, only a few minutes' walk from today's Wimbledon railway station. Today it is a pleasant and busy suburb of London and no sign of the house or its grounds remains but in Nelson's time it was a small hamlet with a population of only around 800 people. Merton Place, the house, had been built towards the end of the 17th century and was purchased on Nelson's behalf in 1801 while he was in the Baltic. Originally of relatively modest proportions, it was extended under Emma Hamilton's direction to become a substantial property with five bedrooms, dressing rooms, servants' quarters, a drawing room, dining room and library, as well as a range of cellars and utility rooms. The estate extended to some 70 acres and a channel led off the nearby River Wandle to provide a landscaped waterway spanned by an Italian style bridge. Nelson first came to live at Merton in 1802 and spent what are often considered the happiest times of his life here until he left for the Mediterranean in May 1803.

After his death at Trafalgar, the house was left unused and Emma Hamilton was forced to sell it (for £12,930) in order to pay off her rapidly mounting debts. It was eventually sold again at auction in 1823 and was later demolished, nothing of the house remaining when the estate was sold off for development in 1846. Since then the whole area has been covered with streets of typical 19th century closely packed houses, while a block of modern council flats stands on the actual site of the house just off Merton High Street. Despite this, a visit to Merton is not an unrewarding experience and, with a bit of patience, there are many Nelson connections to be unearthed. The original estate was originally in two halves, split by the present Merton High Street, joined by a specially constructed underpass. The house stood to the south of the road and its main entrance was near the 'Nelson Arms' public house. Obviously named after the memory of Nelson,

Opposite top:
'The Nelson Arms' at
Merton marks the
approximate site of the
entrance to Nelson's
estate. *ASM*

Above:
The church of St Mary
where Nelson
worshipped while living
at Merton. *ASM*

Left:
The interior of St Mary's
church, Merton. *ASM*

Below left:
Nelson's funeral
hatchment hangs in the
church at Merton. *ASM*

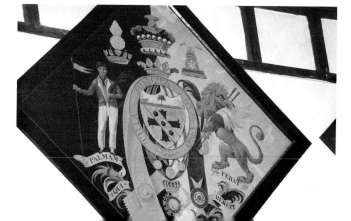

the pub has some excellent tiled mosaic pictures applied to its exterior. On the front are two showing a portrait of Nelson and another of HMS *Victory*. High up on the east facing exterior wall is a most imposing and impressive tile mosaic showing a man-of-war at anchor. Although this is HMS *Victory*, it is a most unusual portrayal as it shows the ship as rebuilt some time after Trafalgar with the waist enclosed and high bulwarks built up around the forecastle. The hull is painted in black and white horizontal stripes, more typical of the mid-nineteenth century style than the yellow and black 'Nelson' style in vogue at Trafalgar.

The rest of the Merton estate was to the north of Merton High Street within an area bounded by Haydons Road, Quicks Road and Merton Road. A stroll around this area quickly reveals the Nelson connection as all the streets within the area described bear associated names. They are, from east to west, Victory Road, Nelson Road, Trafalgar Road, Hardy Road and Hamilton Road. From the west end of the High Street, a walk southwards down Morden Road leads to the Nelson Industrial estate on the right and opposite this is a small park overlooked by a church. This is known as Nelson Park and amongst the carefully tended shrubs stands a granite block bearing a plaque which records the fact that Nelson's house stood nearby. Flanking this modest monument are the barrels of two naval cannon which once stood in Merton Park.

There is yet more to be found, although a little walk is now called for. Follow the A238 (Kingston Road) for half a mile, cross over the railway line and then turn left into Dorset Road. Take the third turning on the right and you will come to the peaceful church of St Mary the Virgin. Here Nelson, who was a devout Christian, came regularly to worship and in fact the very pew on which he and his friends would sit during the service has been restored and stands at the front, nearest to the altar. A small brass plaque records

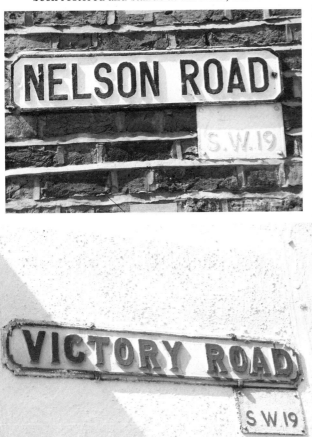

that it was identified and restored by the Nelson Society. On the walls at the side of the nave are hung the funeral hatchments of Nelson and of Sir William Hamilton. Nelson's hatchment has recently been restored and takes the form of a large diamond-shaped panel upon which are painted his Viscount's coat of arms, below which are representations of the medals and decorations which he won. Above the arms are a representation of his Ducal coronet (referring to his Brontë dukedom) together with a traditional naval crown and another bearing the shape of the *San Josef*. The whole device contains numerous references to his life and achievements and is typical of such memorial hatchments produced for famous and noble persons of the period. Sir William Hamilton's hatchment is similar and bears references to his Scottish ancestry.

While Nelson was living at Merton, he made a well-

publicised tour of South Wales and the Midlands, and a number of places bear reminders of their association with him. Starting out a year or so after his triumph at Copenhagen, he combined a number of official duties such as inspecting the dockyard at Milford Haven and carrying out a survey of supplies of timber for shipbuilding in the Forest of Dean with personal interests including a visit to the Worcester works to order a selection of porcelain for his own use and as presents for his family. Among the many places he visited, the ancient town of Monmouth today retains the strongest associations with the events of the past. In fact Nelson stayed here twice, once on the way to Milford Haven and again, a few days later as he journeyed back to England. On the first occasion he arrived by boat along the River Wye on Sunday 4 July 1802, accompanied by his brother and sister-in-law, and the Hamiltons. The party stayed overnight at the 'Beaufort Inn' just off the main square. It was a few weeks later on 18 August that he returned and this time the party stayed for two nights, again at the 'Beaufort Inn'.

Today, the 'Beaufort Arms' (as it is titled) is no longer an inn but this substantial building has been split up into private apartments and the lower-floor contains a shop and an estate agency. However, the front elevation still retains the appearance of an inn although it has been subtly retitled as 'The Beaufort Arms Court'. Passage through an archway to the right leads into what would formerly have been the inn's courtyard where Nelson and his party would have stepped down from their coaches, to be proudly received by the landlord, Mr Watkins. It is recorded that on his first visit, Nelson sat happily after dinner engaged in conversation with Mr Watkins while they demolished a bottle of the latter's best claret! It is perhaps in the courtyard area that today's visitor will best catch a sense of the atmosphere of the times as the view from certain angles is probably unchanged from that which Nelson would have seen.

On the morning of 19 August, Nelson and his party were conveyed by coach and horses up the steep slopes to the south-east of the town in order to visit the Naval Temple, situated at the top of a hill known as the Kymin. Opened by the Duchess of Beaufort on 24 June 1801, the temple took the form of a small seating shelter

Opposite:
Street names off Merton High Street give away the Nelson connection. *ASM*

Above:
This granite block in Nelson Gardens records the existence of Nelson's estate at Merton and is flanked by two cannons which once stood in front of the house. *ASM*

Left:
The courtyard of the 'Beaufort Arms', where Nelson stayed while visiting Monmouth in 1802, appears almost unchanged from that era. *ASM*

Above:
The picturesque Kymin pavilion where Nelson was entertained by the Mayor and and officials of Monmouth. *ASM*

Right:
The Naval Temple at Monmouth, much admired by Nelson, stands near the Kymin pavilion on a hill overlooking Monmouth. *ASM*

Below right:
One of the plaques on the side of the Naval Temple records Nelson's victory at the Nile. *ASM*

THE FIGURE
WHICH CROWNS THE TEMPLE,
EXHIBITS BRITANNIA, SEATED ON A ROCK:
THE PAINTING IN FRONT, REPRESENTS
THE STANDARD OF GREAT-BRITAIN,
WAVING TRIUMPHANT
OVER THE FALLEN AND CAPTIVE FLAGS OF
FRANCE, SPAIN, AND HOLLAND:
THE OPPOSITE SIDE,
THE GLORIOUS AND EVER-MEMORABLE
BATTLE OF THE NILE.

surrounded by a low wall and, today, stands among trees which slightly obscure the view over the Wye Valley and the town of Monmouth several hundred feet below. It commemorates 16 admirals who distinguished themselves against the French and Spanish navies in the period from 1759 to 1801. Each admiral's name is featured on a red, white or blue plaque (the colour relating to the colour of the admiral's flag) and apart from Nelson himself, other illustrious names include Boscawen, Duncan, Hood, Howe, Keith, Rodney and Jervis (St Vincent). The whole edifice is surmounted by a statue of Britannia, while further dedications are inscribed on large plaques on each side wall. During his visit Nelson commented favourably on the fact that it was the only monument of its type to have been erected in the whole of the country.

On reaching the crest of the hill, Nelson was entertained to a celebratory breakfast, hosted by the Mayor and corporation, at the Kymin pavilion which stood a few yards away and also enjoyed the panoramic view. The pavilion, or roundhouse, was built in

Above:
The carefully restored garden pavilion where Nelson took coffee is hidden behind a branch of Lloyd's Bank in Monmouth. *ASM*

Left:
A plaque records that Nelson sat in the garden pavilion. *ASM*

1793 and also stands today and in fact is used as a private dwelling although it belongs, like the temple, to the National Trust. During the 19th century both the Temple and the Kymin were allowed to deteriorate and concern for their upkeep led to their becoming some of the first properties to be adopted by the newly formed National Trust. In 1802, two four-pounder cannon were mounted here and used to fire salutes on special occasions. Needless to say, Nelson's visit warranted the expenditure of a large amount of gunpowder! These guns have long since disappeared.

After breakfasting and visiting the Temple, Nelson insisted on walking back down to the town, an arduous stretch for some of the party. In the evening he was entertained to a civic reception and afterwards went for coffee in a Georgian pavilion situated in the town clerk's garden. This elegant structure is today carefully preserved in an immaculately kept garden belonging to Lloyd's Bank! The pavilion is aligned to face the afternoon and evening sun and the wooden chair in which Nelson sat has been faithfully preserved while a plaque above it commemorates his presence. Unfortunately access to this tranquil spot is restricted, obviously due to the security implications of having large numbers of visitors to the bank's premises. However, public access is permitted on special occasions such as the anniversary of Trafalgar and any application for permission to view the pavilion should be made to the Branch Manager. On my own visit, I found the staff most pleasant and helpful — but then I do have an account at Lloyd's!

Nelson was away from Merton between May 1803 and August 1805 while he tracked the French fleet in the Mediterranean and followed Villeneuve in an epic return chase across the Atlantic. Returning then to England and his home at Merton, he was ashore for only a few weeks before he left for Portsmouth and his final departure aboard HMS *Victory*. Then, as now, Portsmouth was Britain's major naval base but in those days the civilian part of the town was clustered within the massive fortifications which surrounded that dockyard and what is now known as Old Portsmouth. It was to the 'George Hotel' in the High Street that Nelson went when he arrived in Portsmouth early on the morning of Saturday 14 September 1805. After breakfasting he walked to the nearby dockyard where he met various officials and passed on orders to some of his captains before returning to the 'George' and completed his final arrangements before leaving to board the *Victory* which was anchored offshore at Spithead.

By this time word had got around the town that Nelson was preparing to depart and a large crowd had gathered in the High Street and down on the foreshore. Hoping to avoid the press of the crowd, he left by the rear entrance into Farthing Lane, and then into Penny Street which led down past the garrison church to the town's seaward defences. As he walked down the street he was quickly observed and the crowd pressed around making progress

Above:
The 'George Hotel' in the High Street, Old Portsmouth, was demolished many years ago and has been replaced by this unassuming block of apartments. Plaques set in the wall record that Nelson stayed at the 'George' before departing for Trafalgar in September 1805. *ASM*

Opposite:
The upper of these two plaques attached to the wall of the present George Court was originally mounted over an archway in the 'George Hotel' and marks the fact that Nelson passed through it on his way to the *Victory*. *ASM*

ADMIRAL LORD NELSON
PASSED THROUGH THIS ARCHWAY 14th. SEPT. 1805.
ON HIS WAY TO THE SEASHORE TO EMBARK FOR THE LAST TIME.
TO JOIN HIS FLAGSHIP
H.M.S. VICTORY.
AND TAKE COMMAND OF THE
BRITISH FLEET
AT THE GLORIOUS
BATTLE OF TRAFALGAR.

THE ABOVE PLAQUE
WAS FORMERLY OVER
THE PENNY STREET ENTRANCE OF
THE GEORGE HOTEL
WHICH STOOD ON THIS SITE
UNTIL DESTROYED BY ENEMY ACTION IN 1941.
THE PLAQUE
WAS REPOSITIONED HERE IN
1954

difficult. Armed soldiers and marines did their best to clear a way for him as he passed the church and went through the thick ramparts by means of a sally port. From here he walked down to the beach at Southsea and boarded his waiting barge, to be rowed out to his ship with the cheers and encouragement of the crowds ringing in his ears. It was a stirring and memorable scene, especially as Nelson himself seemed aware that he was destined never to return alive.

In retracing Nelson's life, there is nothing quite so fascinating and moving as walking, literally in his last footsteps on land, from the 'George' to the seashore. Although the old High Street retains many buildings from Nelson's time, the 'George Hotel' itself was demolished early in this century and the site is now occupied by a block of flats about half-way down on the south side of the road. The site is easily identified as a plaque set into the front elevation of the flats commemorates the fact that Nelson set off from here on that September day in 1805. Also preserved is part of the archway from a door of the hotel which bears an inscription stating that Nelson passed under it as he left. At the rear of the flats is still the small access lane, Farthing Lane, and Nelson would have walked here on his way into Penny Street which leads down to the foreshore. Many of the buildings in this part of the street have changed little, and walking south-eastwards towards the sea, one still passes the open park on the left, then known as Governor's Green. At the end of Penny Street stood the garrison chapel, now in ruins having been hit by bombs during World War 2. At this point Nelson would have turned to the left, keeping below the ramparts and following the path which led to the sally port, a brick-lined tunnel leading through the walls to a bridge across the moat. All this is still in place today and one can trace his steps exactly.

Once across the moat, he would have stood in the Spur Redoubt, a gun position pointing out into the sea, and from here it was a short walk towards the beach at Southsea where his boat was waiting. The exact site of embarkation is now covered by a funfair, but in Nelson's time there were assembly rooms above the foreshore and a collection of bathing machines on the beach. Just past the fair is a stone plinth surmounted by one of HMS *Victory*'s anchors and this bears inscriptions recording the fact that Nelson departed from near this spot. Although Nelson was destined never to return alive, observers standing on the shore at this point early on 5 December 1805 would have seen the battered *Victory* creeping into the anchorage at Spithead when vast

crowds lined the foreshore in an effort to see the famous ship which carried the body of their revered Admiral.

After lying at Spithead for a week, the ship sailed again for the Downs and the Thames, and Nelson's body was sent ashore to lie in state in the

Painted Hall at the Greenwich Naval Hospital until the day of the great funeral ceremony on 9 January. It was during this voyage up the Channel that the ship's surgeon, Beatty, performed an autopsy on the corpse and removed the fatal bullet which is now on display at the National Maritime Museum. On the day of the funeral, Nelson's body, laid in the coffin made from the timbers of the French flagship at the Nile, *L'Orient*, was conveyed up the Thames in a specially built barge rowed by eight seamen. The coffin was laid on a high covered platform in the stern of the barge, an arrangement which made the craft extremely unwieldy in crosswinds and very difficult to handle. One of the most readable accounts of this melancholy voyage up the Thames to Westminster steps is contained in C. S. Forester's *Hornblower and the Atropos*. Although a work of fiction in which Forester's eponymous hero is placed in command of the funeral barge, the account of the journey and accompanying ceremony is correct and authentic in every detail except that, in Forester's account, Hornblower has to deal with a crisis when the boat springs a leak and is in danger of sinking. Fortunately for history, this did not happen in real life! The actual barge used has been preserved and magnificently restored, and can be seen in the Victory gallery of the Royal Naval Museum at Portsmouth.

Once ashore at Westminster, the coffin was carried in solemn procession to the Admiralty where it lay until the formal procession to St Paul's began later in the day. Although not open to the public, the ante room where the coffin lay is now referred to as the Nelson Room and contains documents, prints and paintings relating to Nelson and his battles. Nearby is the Admiralty board room, the centre of Naval power in the 18th and 19th centuries and still furnished and decorated much as it was at the time of Trafalgar. Over the fireplace at one end of the room is the wind dial, connected to a vane on the roof, which showed the all-important direction of the wind as the board members sat at their meetings. On the opposite wall is one of the most famous and unusual paintings of Nelson by the Italian artist Guzzardi which was painted in Naples after the Battle of the Nile.

At St Paul's Cathedral, the funeral ceremony was of epic proportions with hundreds of invited guests and thousands of onlookers outside. The coffin was lowered into the crypt by mechanical means and today it stands in a sarcophagus mounted on a plinth in a place of honour directly below the centre of the cathedral's great dome. He does not lie alone. Nearby are the graves of some of his brother officers and in alcoves leading off from the central chamber are the graves of other great seaman of more recent wars such as Beatty, Jellicoe and Fraser, while all around are the leaders and heroes of the other fighting services. Above the crypt, in the south wing of the transept, will be found the magnificent memorial to Nelson which bears his statue. Nearby is another great memorial to his lifelong friend Collingwood, while other naval contemporaries are also commemorated. In following the life of Nelson by visiting those places where he lived, worked and played, there is no more fitting climax than to stand quietly in the sombre and magnificent surroundings of London's greatest cathedral and reflect on the man and his sacrifices in the name of his country.

In looking back in this way, the emphasis has been on those sites easily visited today in Britain, but there are many traces of Nelson to be found abroad and while some are almost inaccessible even by the most determined explorer, others can be viewed quite easily in the course of a modern package holiday. Most of his early naval career was spent in the Caribbean and West Indies and, for example, Jamaica holds much of interest. It was here that Nelson was put in command of the garrison troops at Kingston when it was threatened by a French invasion in 1779 and many of the old

Above opposite:
Nelson walked from the 'George' down to his boat waiting on the foreshore at Southsea. His route took him along Penny Street, shown here, and the buildings on the left, and the garrison church in the background, have all survived from that occasion. *ASM*

Opposite:
The sally port leading through the ramparts to the Spur Redoubt at Southsea. Walking through the narrow passageway can be a distinctly eerie experience when recalling that Nelson's last walk on land took him through this very tunnel. *ASM*

fortifications survive. On a hill overlooking Kingston is Admiral's Mountain, the house once occupied by the Commander-in-Chief West Indies, Sir Peter Parker, and his wife and here Nelson stayed for some time recuperating under the eye of Lady Parker after returning from the tragic expedition against Nicaragua in 1780.

At the eastern end of the Caribbean lie the Leeward Islands which held more pleasant memories for Nelson. On Antigua is the naval dockyard (founded in 1725) of English Harbour which he visited on several occasions and would have been very familiar to him. This has been restored in recent years and is very much a tourist attraction with the Nelson connection well to the fore. In fact most of the existing buildings, although quite old, were probably built slightly after Nelson's time but the layout and form of the dockyard have changed little. A few miles away to the west lies the small island of Nevis which was of great significance as it was here that he met and married his wife Frances Nisbet (née Herbert), the widowed daughter of the President of Nevis. The Herberts' house at Montpelier, where the marriage ceremony was performed, has long since been demolished. However, the service was carried out by the Reverend W. Jones, Rector of the Fig Tree church (St John's) which still stands and it is still possible to inspect the faded register of marriages to read the following entry:

'1787. March 11th. Horatio Nelson, Esquire. Captain of His Majesties Ship, the Boreas, to Frances Herbert Nisbet, Widow.'

Apart from the church, a number of stone buildings from Nelson's era survive and a small museum has been opened alongside Government House which houses a collection of Nelson items belonging to an American resident of the island, Mr Robert Abrahams. Holidaymakers visiting the island may well find themselves staying in a purpose-built complex on the 'Nisbet' plantation.

Moving east across the Atlantic, the next place with an important Nelson connection is the island of Tenerife, largest of the Canary Islands lying off the north-west coast of Africa. It was here of course that Nelson led his ill-fated expedition against the port of Santa Cruz on the north-east coast of the island and where he lost his arm in the abortive landings. Although Tenerife is now a popular destination for British holidaymakers, the town of Santa Cruz is well away from the popular beach resorts on the north and south coasts and consequently is not as well known as it might be. However, there is plenty for the Nelson enthusiast to see and it would be well worth hiring a car for a day to make the trip. On the northern edge of the city is the old Paso Alto gun battery which still houses a number of cannon which were employed in the defence of the town in 1797. These have all been given names and one, El Tigre (the tiger), is reputed to be the very

one from which the shot which caused the loss of Nelson's arm was fired. Given the number of guns firing at the time, it is highly unlikely that the precise gun could be identified after the battle — however, it is a nice story and if was not this particular gun, then it was undoubtedly one very much like it. Below the battery, in what were the soldiers' quarters, is a tomb containing the bodies of 23 of the defenders killed in the savage fighting.

Below the battery can be seen the sweep of the bay and the mole which Nelson and his

NEAR THIS MEMORIAL ON THE 14TH SEPTEMBER 1805 ADMIRAL LORD NELSON EMBARKED FOR THE LAST TIME, BEING KILLED ON THE FOLLOWING 21ST OCTOBER AT THE VICTORIOUS BATTLE OF TRAFALGAR.

Opposite:
A monument, incorporating an anchor from HMS *Victory*, stands on the foreshore at Southsea to mark the spot where Nelson embarked for Trafalgar. *ASM*

Above:
The inscription on the Southsea monument. *ASM*

Left:
The beautifully restored ceremonial barge which conveyed Nelson's body up the Thames is today on display at the Royal Naval Museum, Portsmouth. *ASM, by permission Royal Naval Museum*

Below left:
A model on display at the Royal Naval Museum showing the appearance of the funeral barge. The coffin was carried under the canopy in the stern. *ASM, by permission Royal Naval Museum*

men stormed. Although Nelson himself was struck down at the moment he landed, some sailors and marines, under Captain Troubridge, managed to get into the town and fierce fighting took place between what is now Alameda Duque Santa Elena and Barranco de los Santos. Eventually the surviving British were holed up in the convent of Santo Domingo near the Plaza de la Iglesia or else cornered in the Plaza del Principe. One can still walk around these streets and imagine the stirring but desperate events of 200 years ago. With these thoughts in mind, it is a sobering experience to step into the coolness of the church Iglesia de la Conception in the old part of the town which houses the tomb of General Gutierrez, the honourable and brave defender of Santa Cruz when Nelson attacked. On either side are cases containing two British flags captured at the time of the action, one of which is a Union flag of the period while the other is a similar flag but with the name *Emerald* painted in yellow letters across the horizontal bar. This latter flag was presumably taken from a party of seamen and marines landed from the 36-gun frigate *Emerald* and which suffered heavy casualties including their leader, Lt Basham RM.

On a more light-hearted note, there are several bars and cafés around the island which commemorate the name of Nelson including the rather macabrely named 'Nelson's Arm', a bar at Puerto de la Cruz, some 18 miles south of Santa Cruz. This bar adjoins a small Naval Museum which, among various exhibits, has a room devoted to the battle in 1797. There is a fine scale model of the action, together with various accounts and paintings including a portrait of Nelson and one of the *Victory*.

Moving on, much of Nelson's career was spent in the Mediterranean and here there are numerous places which hold memories and associations with the man. In the east is Aboukir Bay on the Egyptian coast, the scene of his first great victory in 1798. There is little to see in the way of artefacts, but the visitor will be able to look out over the bay and perhaps pick out the shoals and shallows which dictated the plan of action. At the other end of the Mediterranean is the island of Corsica where Nelson was heavily involved in action, both on sea and land, in support of operations to capture the island from French forces. The ports of Bastia and Calvi are still flourishing and outlines of their defences can still be seen. It was during the siege of Calvi, while directing the fire of a battery of ships' guns landed ashore, that Nelson received the injuries which resulted in him losing the sight of his right eye. For many years the site of this incident has been marked by a marble plaque on a nearby rock although in recent years a house has been built alongside making access difficult. A visit to the site however shows some of the problems which

Nelson would have had to overcome in order to get his guns in position amongst the rocks of Marcone, to the east of Fort Mozzelo on the outskirts of Calvi. The guns were actually landed at Porto Agro, a small cliff-ensconced cove some two miles from the point at which the guns were required. A walk along the route used to drag the heavy guns on their unwieldy carriages soon illustrates the sheer determination which was required by Nelson and his men to bring them into action. From the rocks at Marcone, the guns kept up a bombardment for almost a month, with every grain of powder and every roundshot having to be brought over the rocky two miles from Porto Agro. Fort Mozzelo was quickly reduced, and fire was then directed on to the Citadel and town.

However, the prime Mediterranean site associated with Nelson must be the city of Naples on Italy's west coast, some 130 miles south of Rome. Nelson first came here on 12 September 1793 when he arrived in command of the *Agamemnon*. Although this romantic city, sited on the shores of a sweeping bay with panoramic views of Mount Vesuvius, Sorrento and Capri, was to become an important centre in his life, this first visit was cut short after only three days as reports of a nearby French force necessitated a hasty departure — breaking a lunch date with no less a personage than the King of Naples. It was to be another five years before he returned, but he had now met the British Ambassador, Sir William Hamilton, and, more significantly, his lively and attractive young wife, Emma. It was to Naples that Nelson came again, battered and exhausted after his victory at the Battle of the Nile, and became inextricably entangled in the complex social and political life of the court of Naples. At the same time his great affair with Emma Hamilton began and the pattern of his life, for better or for worse, was changed for ever.

A visitor to modern Naples is immediately struck by the frantic pace of life as countless people throng the streets, crowding out shops, restaurants, bars and offices. The traffic is a wonder to behold with seemingly limitless numbers of cars, buses, lorries and scooters hurtling along the narrow one-way streets which themselves are almost completely devoid of traffic lights. Those lights which do exist, at pedestrian crossings, are routinely ignored. On all sides, except seawards, the city has expanded in modern times with an ugly sprawl of industrial premises, railway yards, motorways and endless huddles of uninspiring houses and apartment blocks which stretch along the whole shoreline of the bay of Naples with the exception of the southern edge where precipitous cliffs and mountains form a natural containment for the ever growing conurbation. Despite all this, the old centre of the town, based around the Palazzo Reale and the harbour, and stretching up the steep hillside to the Castel Sant'Elmo shows much of the characteristics of an earlier age and it is easy to get lost in a maze of backstreets and alleyways bordered by buildings rising typically to five or six floors as they did in Nelson's time.

Whenever Nelson had occasion to visit Naples, he would usually stay ashore as a guest of Sir William and Lady Hamilton at their residence, the Palazzo Sessa, situated on a hilltop with panoramic views over the bay and only a few minutes' walk from the Royal Court at the Palazzo Reale. The Palazzo Sessa was rented from the Sessa family and still stands today, although it is difficult to view as an entity due to the erection of other buildings on the surrounding

Opposite:
The Palazzo Sessa in Naples, where Nelson met and stayed with Sir William and Lady Hamilton. *ASM*

Above:
A shop near the Palazzo is named after Emma Hamilton. *ASM*

ATE I London Pub.ᵈ March 1ˢᵗ 1794 by Geo.Townly Stubbs Nᵒ 9 High Street Marylebone . OF LADY HAMILTONS ATTITUD

hillside. It is also extremely difficult to find. The best directions are to follow the Via Chaiai from the Palazzo Reale almost as far as the Piazza di Martiri. Just before the Piazza is reached, there is a narrow lane off to the left (Via Capella Vecchia) which is home to several fascinating antique shops. At the top of the lane an archway leads into a private courtyard, on the far side of which is a narrow alleyway which eventually leads straight to the entrance of the Palazzo Sessa. By this time the bustle of urban Naples has been left far behind and the sun is almost completely shut out by the old apartment buildings overlooking the courtyard and alleyway. Entry to the Palazzo is through another archway leading into a small courtyard which is surrounded on the remaining three sides by the towering façades hiding the floors of rooms which saw so much of the excitement, intrigue, diplomacy and socialising which marked Nelson's time here. Access to the Palazzo is almost impossible as it is a very private place although there is a discrete antique shop on the premises and the upper floor is now used as a synagogue. Retracing one's steps to the Via Chaiai, and back into the bright sunshine, stroll down the hill to the Piazza Vittoria near the sea shore and from there it is possible to look back and see a section of the Palazzo Sessa between the elevations of other buildings. A broad shuttered window leading out to a balustraded balcony marks the room where Emma Hamilton would entertain visitors and family with her famous 'Attitudes' — poses, in specially made costumes, with classical allusions. Although well received at the time, later generations must bless the invention of television for family entertainment!

From the Piazza Vittoria, a seafront promenade follows the sweep of the bay westwards towards Posillipo, less than a couple of miles away. It was here that the gentry of the time would have small beach villas which they would use for relaxation and entertainment. Sir William Hamilton was no exception and his Villa 'Emma' was situated just above the beach alongside the Palazzo Donn'Anna which still juts out into the sea at this point. This villa, or casino as it was also termed, was much used by Nelson and Emma Hamilton during his final stay at Naples but today a road running along the clifftop has partially demolished the villa although its remains can be seen at the base of the cliffs where a later building now stands on the original foundations.

Back in the main part of the city many of the buildings and fortifications which played an important role in Nelson's activities are still standing. In the centre are the Palazzo Reale (rebuilt following damage from bombing during World War 2) and the Castel Nuovo, while on the promontory at Santa Lucia is the seemingly impregnable Castel d'Ouvo almost totally surrounded by the sea. Unfortunately Nelson's actions in condoning the hanging of the Neapolitan Admiral Caracciolo following the recapture of Naples in 1799 are remembered with some bitterness in Naples and consequently there was little motivation to preserve anything related to him. There are no statues or plaques and nothing of any consequence in the local museums. A stroll around the area of the Palazzo Sessa and Posillipo will reveal one or two names of houses or businesses which obviously recall the events of two centuries ago, a typical example being the Modestiene 'Emma' — a milliner's shop in an old Palazzo off the Via Chaiai.

There are several other sites of Nelsonian interest in the Mediterranean but space precludes a detailed description. When he was forced to evacuate the Neapolitan royal family from Naples, it was to Palermo on the north coast of Sicily that he sailed. Here he spent some time ashore, while inland is the estate gifted to him when he was awarded the Dukedom of Brontë. In fact he had little time to visit the estate and appointed an agent to look after it and conduct business affairs although he often talked of retiring there with Emma Hamilton. After his death it passed to his family who in recent years sold the estate and the Castello di Maniace to the local authorities. The house still contains furniture, paintings and decorations belonging to Nelson's descendants as they were deemed to be part of Sicily's national heritage and could not be removed when the estate was sold. Elsewhere Nelson must have visited virtually every significant port

Opposite:
Emma Hamilton poses in one of her famous 'Attitudes', often performed to entertain guests at the Palazzo Sessa. *National Maritime Museum*

in the Mediterranean during his many years on the station, particularly those along the coast of Genoa and north-west Italy where he was Commodore of the blockading inshore squadron for some time. At all these places there are fortifications and harbours which, in many cases, have stood the ravages of time. Perhaps the saddest reminder is at Gibraltar where the battered British ships returned after the battle of Trafalgar and landed their many dead who are now buried in the Trafalgar cemetery near the southern end of the rock.

Nelson also came up against powerful land fortifications when he was sent to the Baltic in 1801. The actual site of the battle at Copenhagen has long since disappeared under the modern development of the town and docks, although the area around the Trekroner Fort is now a public park and some of the earthworks and ramparts can still be seen. After the battle, Nelson was involved in delicate negotiations directed towards a permanent ceasefire, and these were carried out at the Amalienborg royal palace which still stands. Across the Baltic, in the Swedish capital of Stockholm, Nelson seems to have made quite an impression even though he never landed there. Within the Gamla Stan, or old town, there are three old buildings now used as hotels and named after Nelson, the *Victory* and Emma Hamilton.

In fact there are few parts of the world where Nelson has not touched and left some small reminder of his presence. To catalogue them all would be virtually impossible, but readers travelling abroad can keep a weather eye open for such reminders. They can be found in the most surprising places.

Above:
The Castel d'Ouvo, on the foreshore at Naples, was one of the forts held by Jacobin forces which surrendered to Nelson when he reoccupied the city in 1799. *ASM*

3: SO WHAT IS LEFT
OF NELSON?

The previous chapters have told the story of Nelson and tried to retrace his life by visiting places associated with him but, to complete the picture, we can go and see objects which actually belonged to him and which he actually held, touched, wore or used. These range from obvious naval items such as swords, medals and uniforms to personal possessions such as plates, furniture and everyday household goods. It is tempting to try and describe these in some sort of chronological order but it would be difficult for readers to go and see things for themselves in the same order as they are mostly held in a variety of different museum collections. Instead, therefore, each of the major collections will be described in turn although this in itself is a major task as some establishments have large and significant displays which also include exhibits relating to people associated with Nelson, both friends and family as well as naval colleagues. In the interest of brevity, only those items of direct relevance are described although it should be remembered that, in most cases, the establishment concerned will probably hold other objects of related interest. Details of all the museums and other places mentioned in this section can be found in a later chapter (Where to see Nelson).

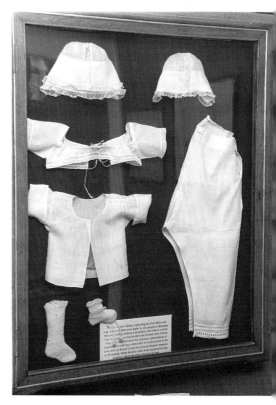

Where to begin? Well a good place would be the Bucklers Hard Maritime Museum, near Beaulieu in Hampshire. This fine museum mainly centres around its shipbuilding connections and pride of place is given to the story of the *Agamemnon* which was built here and was one of Nelson's favourite ships (see Chapter 4). However, what brings us here now is one of the earliest sets of objects associated with the young Nelson — his baby clothes. These are displayed in a wall case and are perfectly preserved. Made in his home village of Burnham Thorpe, they were kept by his family and on his death passed to his Brother, the 2nd Earl. Handed down through descendants, they were presented to the RUSI Museum 1934 (now closed) and passed to Bucklers Hard in 1963. The whole outfit consists of caps and hoods, a shirt, breeches with buttons to allow nappies to be changed, knitted socks and bootees, and a shoulder piece. With the exception of the knitted items, everything is made from white cotton and some are trimmed with lace.

Other Nelson items include an ironstone plate stand and a ring which belonged to him. This has an enamelled decoration showing two white figures on a black background and is one of several of his possessions which were retained by Emma Hamilton after his death, to be later sold off or passed on through her family. From the same source comes a lock of Nelson's hair, its authenticity completely assured, which is more than can be said of many locks of hair, supposedly Nelson's, which turn up occasionally. Finally there is a letter from Nelson to the Admiralty on the rather prosaic subject of rope supplies for the *Agamemnon*. Most museums have originals or facsimiles of letters by Nelson and this is not surprising as he must have written literally thousands in his lifetime. Also to be seen at Bucklers Hard is a bust of Nelson cast with copper taken from his old flagship, the *Foudroyant*. The display is rounded off with a number of prints and engravings together with a pair of pistols, inscribed 'HMS Victory', which belonged to Captain Hardy, his flag captain at Trafalgar.

For a more significant collection of Nelsonia, the next stop must be the Portsmouth Naval Base where Nelson's flagship HMS *Victory* is today preserved. This is described in some detail in the next chapter but, immediately adjacent to the ship, is the Royal Naval Museum which houses an extensive collection portraying the history of the service right up to present times. This is divided into a number of galleries each with a particular theme but of greatest interest so far as this book is concerned is the Lambert McCarthy Gallery named after the American lady who presented her important collection of

A letter written by Lord Nelson on board the *Agamemnon* to the Admiralty asking for 200 fathoms of rope.

Nelsonia to the museum in 1971. These are arranged in cases around the edge of the gallery and are presented in a roughly chronological order, while several important items are displayed in the centre of the room.

On entering the gallery, the first case presents a number of items of general interest including examples of letters written by Nelson and chosen to illustrate the various signatures which he used. The earliest is signed *Horatio Nelson* but subsequent ones show variations which he adopted as he rose in stature and, in particular, was made Duke of Brontë. Thus we see *Nelson*, *Brontë Nelson*, and *Nelson and Brontë*, the latter being the signature which he finally adopted and is found on all his later letters. Also on display is a collection of personal letters written to one Herbert Ross who was a planter in the West Indies and who Nelson met when he served there. Nelson seems to have made great efforts to keep in touch with good friends and the Ross collection covers over 20 years of his writings. The letters are kept in an oak box with silver decorations including a handle made in the form of two cannons and rope, also in silver. Nelson's captain aboard HMS *Lowestoft*, William Locker, also became a lifelong friend and recipient of numerous letters, and ended his career as Governor of the Naval Hospital at Greenwich. Collections of letters such as these have been invaluable to students and biographers of Nelson, providing much first hand information about his thoughts and deeds. A print of Captain Locker is displayed above the collection of letters.

The next case contains a number of items relating to Nelson's time in the West Indies and his marriage to Frances Nisbet, including a facsimile of the wedding certificate (the original is still held in Nevis). A more solid reminder of the occasion is a pocket sundial inscribed *Lat. 17 D:18M*, which is the latitude of the island of

Previous page:
A miniature portrait of Nelson painted by his friend and colleague, Cuthbert Collingwood, while stationed in the West Indies. *National Maritime Museum*

Opposite:
Nelson's baby clothes on display at the Bucklers Hard Maritime Museum. *ASM by permission of the Curator, Bucklers Hard*

Above:
A letter from Nelson written while aboard the *Agamemnon*. *ASM by permission of the Curator, Bucklers Hard*

Left:
A copy of Nelson's famous prayer before Trafalgar. *ASM by permission of the Curator, Bucklers Hard*

Dying request of

LORD NELSON

Addressed to his King and Country on the 21st of October 1805, the glorious day of the Battle of Trafalgar when he so nobly lost his life in their service.

PRAYER BEFORE THE BATTLE
written by Lord Nelson at 7 O'clock in the morning "the enemy wearing in succession".

May the Great God whom I worship, grant to my country, and for the benefit of Europe in general, A great and glorious victory! and may no misconduct in any one tarnish it! and may humanity after victory be the predominant feature in the British Fleet. For Myself individually I commit my life to him who made me, and may his Blessing light upon my endeavours for serving my country faithfully. To him I resign myself and the just cause which is entrusted me to defend. Amen Amen Amen

© George Johnson 1886

Nevis where the marriage took place, one of many gifts presented to the happy couple. Also shown is a one of Nelson's visiting cards, inscribed *Capt. Nelson Royal Navy*, and a copy of the 1792 edition of the Navy List showing Nelson's promotion to the rank of Post Captain as being effective from 11 June 1779. There are also a number of documents relating to Lady Nelson including a letter written by her using the signature *Nelson and Brontë* and a copy of the Act of Parliament granting Lady Nelson a pension after the death of her estranged husband.

Next we come to a display relating the story of Nelson's infatuation and relationship with Emma Hamilton. There are several prints showing the couple and also their house at Merton in Surrey but, more importantly, there is the very first letter, dated August 1798, which Nelson ever wrote to her. In addition there are a number of other pieces of correspondence written by Emma Hamilton and another from Sir William Hamilton. Of great interest is a prayer book which originally belonged to Captain Locker but which he presented in 1779 to Nelson who, in turn, gave it to Emma Hamilton before leaving for Trafalgar. The book has been signed by all three and is consequently unique. This part of the display is completed by some sections of a hem from one of Emma Hamilton's dresses, but further along another case contains a brown silk embroidered tunic dress which is thought to have belonged to their daughter, Horatia, although it shows signs of having been altered from a style popular around 1793 and could possibly therefore have been worn originally by Emma Hamilton herself.

In a separate case is a wonderful display of objects which belonged to Nelson or were kept by members of his family. The whole collection came to the museum from Maurice Suckling Ward who was the youngest grandson of Horatia, and the last of Nelson's great grandsons. Included are some striking miniature paintings, exquisitely mounted, of many of the characters in Nelson's life including Sir William Hamilton, Emma Hamilton, Mrs Cadogan (Emma's mother), his daughter Horatia, and some of himself. There are also paintings of Horatia, one of which shows her as a child of two and was kept by Nelson in his cabin aboard the *Victory*. As with any father, Nelson doted on his daughter and an example of this is a silver gilt cup engraved 'Horatia, To much loved Horatia 21 August 1805, Nelson and Brontë', purchased as a gift shortly before he set off on his last voyage.

There are a number of items relating to his experiences with the Court of Naples including the Maltese cross awarded to Emma Hamilton when she was made Dame Petite Croix of the Order of St John of Jerusalem by Czar Paul of Russia in 1799. In passing it should be mentioned that she was often referred to as Lady Hamilton, but this courtesy title derived from her husband's status as an English knight and in no way resulted from her connection with Nelson or any foreign awards. Of Nelson's personal effects there are a pair of silver candlesticks inscribed with a coronet and the initial 'N', a bracelet made from his hair, a chiming gold watch, a silver gilt cup given to him by Emma Hamilton and a number of rings including one of gold inscribed 'Nelson and Brontë'. There are also gold rings belonging to Emma Hamilton and a gold and pearl locket with a miniature of Nelson, containing a lock of his hair cut off after his death at Trafalgar.

The next few cases provide a stunning example of the way Nelson mania swept the country in the early 19th century. There are all sorts of representations of the man including miniature paintings, busts, various types of plaques by Wedgwood and many statues and figures. Of the latter, several are of brightly coloured Staffordshire ware which today are avidly sought by collectors and fetch several hundred pounds, a popular subject being groups of figures representing the Death of Nelson. There is a vast collection of commemorative pieces including glassware, jugs, dishes, cups and mugs, some of which were produced at the beginning of this century for the Trafalgar centenary celebrations in 1905. Space prohibits a detailed description of all these items and readers are urged to make the effort to see this collection for themselves.

Further cases contain yet more of Nelson's possessions briefly described below, but a personal visit is recommended in order to take in all that is here. In Nelson's time the presentation of silver was a common way of marking the actions and deeds of prominent men and, in his lifetime, Nelson acquired a considerable collection. Among the items on view at Portsmouth are a pair of silver hotplates (on loan from the Admiralty), a pair of gimballed candlesticks from his cabin aboard HMS *Victory*, and a carving set engraved 'N&B'. There is also some glassware comprising a set of six nesting tumblers, sugar bowls, and two large tumblers, as well as various pieces of porcelain including a pair of lidded vases with red and gold decor and a washbowl set. A number of his books still survive including a Spanish Grammar and another on navigation theory entitled *The Longitude Found*, this latter a gift from his uncle, Maurice Suckling. Other possessions include a quadrant made by Richard Hornby and inscribed 'Horatio Nelson RN 1793', a silver snuff box bearing his coat of arms, a visiting card bearing the words 'Viscount Nelson, Duke of Brontë', a private seal for use with letters and documents, a pair of shoe buckles and a rather unusual silver toothpick with a retractable blade.

In a corner of the gallery is a substantial collection of furniture which belonged to Nelson, some of it designed for use aboard ship where it was necessary that each item could be quickly broken down into easily managed sections so that it could be stowed away when the ship cleared for action. Designed in this manner by Richard Gillow are a folding dining table and a modular sideboard. Other items which he would have used at sea include a writing slope with compartments for storing paper, pens and ink, and some sea chests used to carry clothes and his dinner service. One fascinating piece is a huge wine cooler, its size accounted for by the fact that sea water, and not ice, was used to chill the wine. To complete the display are one or two items from Nelson's house at Merton including some pieces of china. Although Nelson spent a considerable time at sea, it can be imagined from some of the items seen here that his style of life was not altogether spartan, particularly in the Mediterranean where the summer climate was generally pleasant, allowing the ships to be dry and well ventilated.

Opposite:
This blue and white Staffordshire plate is typical of the many contemporary items produced to commemorate Nelson. It depicts the moment he was struck down on the quarterdeck of HMS *Victory*. *ASM, by permission Royal Naval Museum*

Above:
A bronze bust of Nelson by Alexander Graham on display at the Royal Naval Museum. *ASM, by permission Royal Naval Museum*

The Royal Naval Museum has on show a number of important portraits of Nelson by a variety of artists. These include examples by Lemuel Abbott painted in 1798, Simon de Koster in 1800 and Arthur Devis in 1805. The latter was done after Nelson's death from sketches made by the artist while the *Victory*'s surgeon performed a post mortem on the body! On the other hand, the de Koster portrait is often held to be the one that Nelson himself though to be the best likeness. Other paintings include one by Hoppner, painted around 1800/1801 and acknowledged to be one of the most accurate by contemporaries, and another by Friedrich Heinrich Fuger, painted in Vienna when Nelson visited the city on his way home from Naples in 1801.

Perhaps the most intriguing exhibits are cast masks of Nelson's face. Originally these were thought to have been death masks, taken for a permanent likeness after Nelson died. Gruesome as it may sound, this was a common practice at the time before photography made such measures unnecessary. However, following research in recent years, it is now almost certain that one of these masks was taken in Vienna while Nelson was obviously alive and consequently provides an authentic guide to his appearance and features. Of the two on display, one has a particularly bizarre history, having been found in an Isle of Wight antique shop by Queen Mary, the wife of King George V, in 1936! The life mask from Vienna on show here has closed eyes, but there is a similar one at the National Maritime Museum with the eyes open.

Nelson's battles are well represented by displays of prints, paintings and commemorative medals, but there is nothing of a personal nature except

for a letter written by a Lt George Brown aboard *Victory* at Trafalgar, attached to which are two hairs which he claims come from Nelson's head. In following the Nelson trail, it is amazing how much of his hair is still around — even within this museum are bracelets and rings woven from hair cut off while he was still living! After he died, there was the great state funeral and service at St Paul's and this is marked by a display of related ephemera including booklets and sheets giving the order of service and the various hymns and anthems, a mourning locket, music scores, and a ticket for a Lt Thomas Wing RM to participate in the procession. Finally there are several prints of the death of Nelson.

In addition to the Lambert McCarthy Gallery described above, the Royal Naval Museum also incorporates the Victory Gallery which, as its name implies, is

mostly concerned with aspects of the ship itself but also provides much useful background material as well as one or two personal items. There are some letters written by Nelson to Lord Barham and Captain Blackwood, as well as sailing orders signed by him and addressed to the ships *Britannia* and *Leviathan*. There is a silver salt cellar, inscribed with the *San Josef* motif much favoured by Nelson, and also some plates from one of his dinner services which also feature the same design. A glass decanter on show was given by Nelson to Admiral Graves, his second-in-command at the Battle of Copenhagen. Also to be found are several relics, including a telescope, seals and a prayer book, relating to Captain John Pascoe who rose to command the *Victory* in 1842. In 1805 he was Nelson's signal lieutenant at the Battle of Trafalgar and it was he who suggested that the word 'expects' should be used in Nelson's famous signal instead of 'confides' which Nelson had suggested originally. The change was made as it would entail the use of fewer signal flags. Some items on display have been removed from HMS *Victory* and include the ship's wheel, mounted in 1806 to replace the one damaged at Trafalgar, and the original brass plaque mounted on the deck to show the spot where Nelson fell, the one on the ship today being a replica.

A small side gallery contains material relating to the officers and men who fought alongside Nelson at Trafalgar and there are, for example, several items belonging to Captain Hardy. After Trafalgar he rose to become First Sea Lord in 1830 and on show here are his decanter box with eight decanters and glasses, a sextant, watch and telescope, a small two barrelled percussion pistol, buckles, and a powder flask. Many of the medals won by men at Trafalgar are on show here, while medals and awards for other actions are on display in the main part of the Victory Gallery. The upper floor of the gallery is given over to a display covering the general history of the sailing warship in the Royal Navy but suspended in the centre is the very barge used to convey Nelson's body up the Thames from Greenwich to Westminster on the day of his funeral.

While in Portsmouth, a visit to the Royal Marine Museum at Eastney is to be recommended as this also contains a display featuring the Battle of Trafalgar and has a few pieces of Nelson ephemera. Inevitably there is one of his letters — this one, written in 1804, on the subject of the duties of the Marine gunners under his command at Deal. There are a number of prints and a good collection of the various commemorative medals struck by Davison awarded to the participants at the Battle of Trafalgar. A particularly unusual exhibit is a sketch made by 2nd Lt Reeves aboard HMS

Above opposite:
A magnificent blue and gold tea set from Nelson's home at Merton stands on a sideboard which could be disassembled for stowing aboard ship. *ASM, by permission Royal Naval Museum*

Opposite:
One of several versions of the famous Lemuel Abbott portrait of Nelson, painted while he was recovering from the loss of his right arm. *ASM, by permission Royal Naval Museum*

Above:
A portrait of Nelson by Simon de Koster, painted in 1800. It is generally held that Nelson himself thought this portrait was the most accurate likeness of him. *ASM, by permission Royal Naval Museum*

Victory showing the disposition of ships at noon on the day of battle. In similar vein is a watercolour, one of three, showing the Battle of the Nile and painted by Captain James Weir RM who was present at the battle. These are the only surviving pictorial records made at the time.

At the Battle of Trafalgar, when the deck of the *Victory* came under fire from French marksmen in the rigging of the *Redoubtable,* Nelson ordered Captain Adair, in command of the *Victory*'s Marine detachment, to take a party aloft and clear the enemy out. As he started to climb the rigging he was shot and killed, only moments before Nelson himself was hit. There is a considerable collection of Captain Adair's possessions and documents on show at the museum including his pistol, which was not found until 1846 when repairs were being made to what was his cabin aboard the *Victory*. Although the wooden butt had rotted away, a new one was made from oak timbers taken from the ship.

Interesting though these displays at Portsmouth may be, it is the National Maritime Museum at Greenwich which holds the largest collection of Nelson-related objects and memorabilia, not all of which is always on display due to problems of space. In fact the Museum will often loan out items to other establishments so that they are not entirely lost from public view. At Greenwich the extensive Nelson collection is displayed in the Nelson Gallery on the first floor of the museum's West Wing and the visitor should allow a considerable amount of time to take in all the aspects of this fabulous display. Like the Naval Museum at Portsmouth, there is some attempt to present the exhibits in some form of chronological order, but given the sheer scale of the collection, this is difficult. There is, for a start, a magnificent collection of paintings, both of Nelson and his battles, and also of friends, relatives and others who played a significant role in his life. In the latter category come portraits of Vice-Admiral Collingwood, his second-in-command at Trafalgar, by Henry Howard; Sir Henry Blackwood, senior frigate commander at Trafalgar, by Hoppner; Sir William Beatty, the *Victory*'s surgeon, by Arthur Devis; Captain J. Cooke, commanding the *Bellerophon* at Trafalgar, by Lemuel Abbott; Troubridge, one of his favourite captains, as a Rear-Admiral of the White by Sir William Beatty; Hardy as a Rear-Admiral in 1832 by Richard Evans and another of him as Captain of HMS *Triumph* in 1809 by Domenico Pellegrini; and Captain Locker, his commander aboard HMS *Lowestoft*, by Gilbert Stuart. There is also a rare painting of Nelson's wife,

Frances, as the Viscountess Nelson by an anonymous artist and, by contrast, another of Emma Hamilton posing as Ariadne by the well-known artist George Romney.

Of Nelson himself, there are too many to list here in detail but virtually every well-known portrait of the man can be seen here. The earliest known portrait was painted by John Francis Rigaud (1742-1810) for whom Nelson sat as a young Lieutenant in 1776, although the painting was not finished until 1781 by which time Nelson had been promoted to Captain, requiring some alterations to the work. Another well-known work is that painted by Lemuel Abbott while Nelson was convalescing at the Greenwich Naval Hospital after losing his right arm in 1797 and in the portrait can be seen the tapes on the sleeve of his jacket that were undone when the wound needed to be dressed. Confusingly, Abbott produced several variations of this painting, using it as a basis for later portraits, and these will be found in other museums (one in the Royal Naval Museum has already been mentioned). One of these is perhaps the best known of Nelson, showing him after the Battle of the Nile with all his decorations and the fabulous jewelled Chelengk in his hat, and this is also hung at Greenwich. A more unusual portrait shows Nelson standing and wearing the full dress uniform of a Rear Admiral and

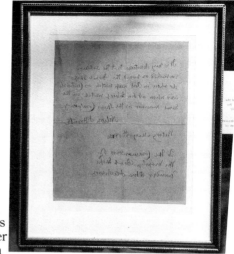

was painted by the Italian Leonardo Guzzardi in Naples shortly after the Battle of the Nile. The style is unlike any of the English renderings, both in the pose and the details of the clothing, while the face bears a rather pained expression — not surprising as Nelson had received a serious head wound during the battle. Again, there are several versions of this painting and another hangs in the board room of the Admiralty (now part of the MoD) at Whitehall.

Although painted after Nelson's death, there is a series of stirring pictures which are the work of Richard Westall (1756-1836). These portray various incidents in Nelson's life including a well known one showing him as a young midshipman facing up to a polar bear while taking part in the Arctic expedition of 1773. Others show him boarding a prize as a lieutenant from HMS *Lowestoft*, receiving the surrender of the *San Nicolas* at the Battle of St Vincent, the encounter with the Spanish launch off Cadiz in 1797, and his wounding at Tenerife later that year. The circumstances of Nelson's tragic death at Trafalgar are covered by several artists, of which the most spectacular and well known are those by Denis Dighton (1792-1827), Samuel Drummond (1765-1844) and Arthur

Opposite:
A plan of the battle of Trafalgar drawn by a Royal Marine officer present at the battle and now displayed at the Royal Marine Museum, Eastney. *ASM, by permission of the Curator*

Above:
Letter written by Nelson in 1804 concerning the duties of Marine gunners. *ASM, by permission of the Curator, RM Museum*

Above left:
A well-known portrait of Emma Hamilton by George Romney. *National Maritime Museum*

Devis (1763-1822). The first of these shows Nelson as he falls, mortally wounded, to the deck of the *Victory* while the battle rages around him and the second portrays him at the top of a ladder as he is carried from the deck to the cockpit below. The most famous image is Devis' *The Death of Nelson* showing him lying in the dim cockpit surrounded by anxious and grieving members of the crew. Devis visited the *Victory* as she returned to England and spent a considerable time on board, sketching the interior of the cockpit and obtaining likenesses of all the survivors involved. Consequently, although there is a certain amount of artistic licence in the composition of the picture, it is an extremely accurate and fascinating piece of work. Alongside the painting is a description of the scene which identifies the several figures surrounding Nelson as he breathed his last.

On a lighter vein, in another part of the gallery will be found two small amateurish paintings; one of Nelson done by his friend Collingwood when they served in the West Indies and another of Collingwood by Nelson himself. These are charming likenesses but it must be said that Collingwood's work is much better than Nelson's!

As would be expected there are also numerous paintings of Nelson's battles, several by front rank artists, and pride of place goes to a massive canvas of the battle of Trafalgar by Joseph Mallord William Turner (1775-1851), one of the most influential of all British artists. The painting was commissioned by King George IV in 1823 to be hung in St James's Palace and was later donated to the Greenwich Hospital in 1829. In typical Turner style, the painting does not set out to show the battle in factual detail but aims to capture the power and atmosphere of the event. Of the other battles there are two of Copenhagen, one by Robert Dodd showing the British fleet forcing its way through the narrows abreast the Kronburg Castle, and the other by John Thomas Serres showing the battle in progress. The Battle of the Nile is covered by a painting showing the destruction of the *L'Orient* (a well-known image) by George Arnald (1763-1841) and another, showing a general view of the battle by Nicholas Pocock (1741-1821). The latter artist specialised in accurate representations of naval battle scenes and there are several other examples of his work to be seen including one entitled 'Nelson's Flagships' showing an imaginary scene in which the *Agamemnon, Vanguard, Foudroyant, Captain* and *Victory* are at anchor together. This was commissioned as a illustration for the first official biography of Nelson by McArthur and Clarke.

There are several other paintings to be seen in the Nelson Gallery, and these are complemented by a comprehensive collection of prints, aquatints and engravings which cover every aspect of Nelson's life and death. One of the best of these, and one which covers a subject not illustrated by paintings, is an aquatint of the interment of Nelson at St Paul's. This is the work of F. C. Lewis after an original line drawing by Charles Pugin.

As far as actual relics of Nelson are concerned, it is difficult to know where to begin. Perhaps the most obvious and eye-catching are his uniforms and other items of clothing, some of which he actually wore at Trafalgar. The finest is a full dress Vice-Admiral's coat with gold lacing of the lapels, pockets, collar and skirt, and bearing the two rings of rank on the sleeves. On the left breast are

Opposite:
The National Maritime Museum has many portraits of Nelson by various artists. This rather unusual example is by he Italian Leonardo Guzzardi and was painted at Naples shortly after the Battle of the Nile.
National Maritime Museum

Above:
The uniform coat from Nelson's full dress uniform showing the insignia of a Vice-Admiral. Note the gold lacing which trims the front, collar, pockets and edges of the coat. On the left breast are the insignia of his orders. *National Maritime Museum*

the stars and insignia of his four orders which adorned all his uniforms. At the Battle of Trafalgar he wore the undress version of this uniform, a more practical version for everyday wear, and this is preserved at Greenwich today, still showing the hole in the left shoulder where the fatal bullet entered, carrying away part of the shoulder epaulette with it. Although the undress uniform was adorned with less gold lace, it still marked him out as a senior officer, particularly as it was also adorned with the insignia of his four orders. At Trafalgar, his fellow officers vainly attempted to persuade him to cover these glittering adornments during the battle but he refused and it is quite possible that this resulted in him being singled out as a target by the French marksmen. Apart from the coat, there are several other items of clothing which he wore at the time of his death including a bloodstained waistcoat, and breeches and stockings. The latter two items were cut off as he lay in the cockpit so that he could be examined by the surgeon and were retained for posterity by one of the *Victory*'s Marine officers. To complete this collection is another of Nelson's uniform coats, this time from his undress uniform as a Rear-Admiral and worn at the Battle of the Nile in 1798. Visitors' attention is drawn to the grease marks on the collar, caused by his pigtail of hair which hung over it. In fact Nelson's very pigtail and its bindings (yes, more hair!) is also on display here, in a section dealing with his death and funeral. This pigtail was cut off by Hardy and presented to Emma Hamilton, later being given to Greenwich Hospital in 1881 by one of her grandchildren. In another section of the display is a pair of stockings, white, with blue vertical stripes, worn by him at the time he was injured during the attack on Tenerife.

Alongside the uniforms is the actual musket ball which killed Nelson. This was removed by the surgeon, Beatty, and later presented to Captain Hardy. It is now mounted in a crystal carried on a pendant, and pieces of gold bullion and cloth from Nelson's uniform coat are still attached to it. Alongside is a copy of a book written by Beatty in 1807, entitled *The Authentic Narrative of the Death of Lord Nelson*, and this is open at the page showing a detailed sketch of the wound and the bullet itself. Copies of this book are not uncommon and will often be found in other museums.

There is a comprehensive display of ephemera concerning the funeral itself which includes sheet music, tickets, contemporary newspaper reports, prints, and a copy of the order of service. A more solid reminder is the figurehead, carved from the timbers of HMS *Victory*, of the actual funeral carriage. There is also shown one of 58 memorial rings commissioned after Nelson's death and presented to various officials and members of his family. These are gold with enamelled decoration

featuring two coronets representing his Viscountcy and the Dukedom of Brontë, and carrying the inscription '21st October 1805 aged 47'. Examples of these rings will be found in several other museums and private collections and some open up to show a lock of his hair.

As would be expected, there is a comprehensive display of material relating to the Battle of Trafalgar including etchings, models and newspaper reports. Of first hand interest is a telescope belonging to the *Victory*'s signal officer, Lt Pascoe, which now carries an inscription that it was actually used aboard the *Victory* at the battle. There are also facsimile copies of Nelson's diary and journal with entries including his famous last prayer and the codicil to his will where he entrusted Emma Hamilton and his child to his King and Country. The museum holds original copies of all these, but they are deemed too valuable to be on public display.

At the western entrance to the Nelson Gallery is a case with several reminders of his early life including a copy of the Bible in two volumes contained in a wooden case. These were given to Nelson by his godmother, Sarah Hope, in 1762 and on the brass clasp of the case is the inscription 'To my dear Godson, Horatio Nelson, The Parsonage, Burnham Thorpe, Norfolk'. Also shown is a midshipman's dirk and an etching by J. Clevely showing the ketches *Racehorse* and *Carcass* trapped in ice during the 1773 Arctic expedition which Nelson accompanied at the age of 15.

The Battle of the Nile was Nelson's first major victory as a fleet commander and is well represented. One of the most intriguing exhibits is the lightning conductor from the main royal masthead of the French flagship, *L'Orient*, which blew up and sank during the engagement. This piece was subsequently salvaged and presented to Nelson who kept it, with many other trophies, at his Merton home. After the battle, the jubilant captains of the British ships formed a so-called Egyptian or Crocodile Club and commissioned the making of several swords to mark the victory. These featured a hilt in the shape of a crocodile and one, suitably inscribed and with the crocodile made out of gold, was presented to Nelson, while their own were of a similar design but with a hilt of gilt and enamel. One of these is on show and is engraved with the crest of Sir Samuel Hood, commander of the *Zealous 74*. As with all of Nelson's victories, a tremendous range of commemorative items were produced and an excellent selection is on display including Prattware jugs, and Staffordshire and Sunderland pottery in addition to various prints and engravings.

As a result of this victory, Nelson was showered with gifts and decorations. A particularly generous admirer was Selim III, the Sultan of Turkey, who sent a magnificent musket featuring an ivory stock inlaid with gold and diamonds, a drinking canteen also decorated with gold, and a scimitar, again exquisitely made and decorated. However, the most valuable and remarkable gift from the Sultan was a staggering piece of jewellery known as the

Above opposite:
A close-up view of the insignia of the four orders bestowed on Nelson and which he proudly displayed at all times. Uppermost is the British Order of the Bath, in the centre are the Neapolitan Order of St Ferdinand and Merit and the Turkish Order of the Crescent, and below is the Maltese cross of the Order of St Joachim awarded by the German States. *National Maritime Museum*

Opposite:
The actual undress Vice-Admiral's uniform coat worn by Nelson when he was struck down at Trafalgar. The hole torn in the material on the left shoulder and the damage to the shoulder epaulette show the point at which the musket ball tore into his body. *National Maritime Museum*

Above:
Copies of the book written by the *Victory*'s surgeon, William Beatty, are on display at several museums and are generally open at the page showing details of the bullet which killed Nelson. *ASM, by permission of the Curator, Bucklers Hard*

Chelengk. The award of this from a Muslim ruler was the equivalent of the highest awards of chivalry in the Christian world and this was the first time that it had ever been presented to anyone outside Islam. The decoration itself consisted of a central large diamond with a diamond-encrusted surround and mounting, above which where 13 'rays', made up of more diamonds. The central diamond was made to rotate by a hidden clockwork mechanism so that it would further reflect the light. Nelson was naturally very excited by this award and wore it in his hat as part of his uniform on important occasions. After his death it passed to his brother, William , and was kept by his family until the 1920s when it was sold off and bought for the nation, ending up at Greenwich. Unfortunately it cannot be seen today as it was stolen in 1951, although the other gifts are still on display. However, a replica of the Chelengk was made in 1973 for use in a film, and this is held by the museum and can be viewed by special arrangement.

Another of Nelson's battle souvenirs is a ship's bell from the Spanish first rate, the 112-gun *San Josef*, which he captured at the Battle of St Vincent. This ship, as was common practice at the time, was repaired after the battle and taken into Royal Navy service, even serving briefly as a flagship for Nelson himself at one point. The bell was subsequently used by HMS *Ganges*, a shore training establishment on the east coast, and was passed on to the museum when it closed down in the 1960s. The old *San Josef* finished her days as a floating gunnery school and was broken up in 1849 but from some of her salvaged timbers was made a magnificent hexagonal table and this now stands in the centre of the museum's Nelson Gallery — a really tangible link with the past as visitors can actually touch and feel it!

Displayed in other cases are parts of the magnificent porcelain tea and dinner services which Nelson acquired in later years for use on board ship and for his home at Merton. Perhaps the finest is a Worcester service ordered from the Chamberlain factory in 1802 to their Japanese design, No 240, which features a mainly floral pattern in dark blues, oranges and reds, all outlined and inlaid with gold. Into the basic pattern are

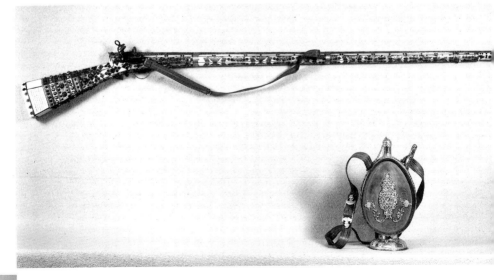

worked various symbols associated with Nelson including coronets, the Chelengk and the stern profile of the *San Josef*. On display are examples of plates, bowls, cups, saucers, dishes and even eggcups, all in this rich and stunning design. More prosaic, but still of great interest, are examples from the so-called 'Baltic' set which is a much plainer design and on the plates consists of a laurel of oak leaves and acorns around the rim with an anchor motif in the centre. Around the plate are inscriptions commemorating the Battles of St Vincent, the Nile and Copenhagen. Some of the larger items in this service such as bowls and serving dishes bear Nelson's coat of arms, with its supporters of a seaman and a lion, in the centre. A set of similar design featuring the oak leaf and anchor motifs, was commissioned by Nelson as a gift for his brother-in-law, George Matcham, and examples of this are referred to as the 'Matcham' set.

As already related, Nelson was given several valuable awards of silver to mark his achievements and the National Maritime Museum has an extensive representative collection on display including items awarded by Lloyd's of London after his victories at the Nile and Copenhagen. These include forks and spoons dated 1796 and 1800 by Eley and Fearn of London, four small bowls (salts) by Robert and David Hennel (London 1799), a coffee pot and stand (Hennel, 1799), a pair of coasters (also Hennel, 1800), plates by Timothy Renou (1801), a pair of inscribed wine coolers (1801) and a pair of sauce boats by Daniel Pontifex.

Strangely enough, despite the acquisition of these and other treasures, Nelson was never a rich man. Unlike many of his contemporaries, he made little prize money, and he had to borrow heavily to buy his house and estate at Merton. This is the subject of another section of the display which features items relating to Merton and includes several pieces of furniture of which the most

Opposite:
The fabulous diamond-encrusted Chelengk was worn by Nelson in his hat and often features in portraits. The original was stolen from the National Maritime Museum in 1951. *National Maritime Museum*

Below opposite:
An exquisitely decorated musket and drinking canteen, part of a series of gifts bestowed on Nelson by Selim III of Turkey after the Battle of the Nile. *National Maritime Museum*

Above:
A small selection of pieces from the magnificent Worcester 'Japanese' dinner service commissioned by Nelson in 1802. *National Maritime Museum*

Above left:
A plate from one of Nelson's dinner services bearing his coat-of-arms in the centre and commemorating the Battle of St Vincent and the capture of the *San Josef* around the edge. *National Maritime Museum*

notable is a semicircular four-legged painted hall table, above which is a decorated framed mirror incorporating Nelson's coat of arms. There are also a pair of wooden chairs with a wicker seat and fine carved arms, a set of nesting tables, and a pair of wall candelabra. Several engravings of Nelson and Emma Hamilton can be seen, and contemporary visitors to Merton reported that in every room the walls were hung with such items together with reminders and souvenirs of his various battles.

Among the more personal objects on display are a leather glove belonging to Nelson, a small tortoiseshell box belonging to Emma Hamilton and carrying a crystal intaglio on the lid in the likeness of Nelson, and an enamel mosaic necklace worn by both Emma Hamilton and her daughter, Horatia. Also to be seen here is Horatia's plain gold wedding ring and a gold necklace with a dog pendant hanging on it. Apparently Horatia once expressed a liking for dogs and Nelson bought a puppy for her but it disappeared soon afterwards. He therefore bought her the gold dog and necklace, remarking that it was less likely to wander off! Another unusual and very personal item which always attracts interest is a knife and fork combined into a single implement, together with its case. This was used by Nelson after the loss of his right arm at Santa Cruz and is, therefore, designed for a left-handed man.

It really is not possible to describe the whole of the National Maritime Museum's collection within the confines of this chapter and, although some of the main items are described above, there is much more to see. The museum is continually expanding its collection and new items are regularly coming to light. Some of these new acquisitions are temporarily displayed in a separate case and include rings belonging to Emma Hamilton and a number of gifts to her daughter Horatia in the period after Nelson's death. In the grounds outside the main building will be found various pieces of ordnance from the Nelson era, while across the road is the original Greenwich Hospital, now the Naval Staff College, with its magnificent painted hall, open to the public, where Nelson lay in state before being borne up the Thames for his funeral in January 1806.

Apart from Portsmouth and Greenwich, the other major collection of Nelsonia open to the public is at the Welsh market town of Monmouth. As described in the previous chapter, Nelson visited the town in 1802 and this may have been the inspiration for Lady Llangattock to begin her famous collection now housed in the town museum. Here Nelson's life and death are described in well laid out displays featuring prints, watercolours and facsimiles of contemporary documents. The scale of this display is smaller than those at the other museums and it is perhaps easier to study the exhibits in a relatively quiet atmosphere. One display case is of particular interest and provides cause for some amusement as it concentrates on various forgeries and fakes resulting from the insatiable demand by collectors for objects purporting to be associated with Nelson. Some of these are described later.

As far as genuine articles are concerned, among the most interesting are several swords including Nelson's own fighting sword which was purchased just before he sailed on his final voyage and was sent home to Emma Hamilton after his death. It was subsequently acquired, along with a number of Nelson's other possessions, by an Alderman Smith and later passed to his servant, John Kinsey. In 1847 Kinsey tried to sell the sword and an advertisement appeared in the national press but apparently he was unable to obtain a reasonable price and it was pawned. Rescued from this ignominious fate by an innkeeper from Bushey, it later passed via a Mrs Trehorne into the Llangattock collection. The sword has an overall length of 30.5in, a fact alluded to in a handwritten note by John Kinsey currently in the possession of the museum. Also displayed is a copy of the newspaper advertisement offering the sword for sale in 1847. Nelson's Dress Sword has long since disappeared, but a remarkable coloured sketch of it exists on the back of an invoice issued by the London swordsmiths Barrett & Corney to whom it was entrusted for repairs to the hilt in 1805. The invoice is endorsed as having been settled only a week before Nelson sailed for Trafalgar.

Also at Monmouth are two other dress swords which, although not Nelson's, have a dramatic association with him as they were those belonging to the commanding admirals of the defeated French and Spanish fleets at Trafalgar. The first belonged to Admiral Villeneuve, the overall commander of the Combined fleets, and is a double-edged weapon with an ornate pommel and a silver wire grip. Attached to the sword is a medal which bears the inscription 'Sword of Admiral Villeneuve, Commander in Chief of the Combined Fleets of France and Spain. Surrendered to Lord Collingwood, October 21st 1805'. The other sword belonged to Rear-Admiral Cisneros who was one of the Spanish commanders during the battle and this has a steel blade with a finely embossed grip. Accompanying the sword is also a medal (both probably made in 1821/22) bearing the inscription 'Don Baltazar Hidalgo Cisneros, Spanish Rear-Admiral taken in the Santissima Trinidad. October 21st 1805'.

As with the other museums, Monmouth has a comprehensive collection of silverware and porcelain belonging to Nelson. There are examples of pieces from the Chamberlain, Baltic and Matcham sets while the silver includes a silver casket dating from 1799 and inscribed 'To the Hero of the Nile from Sir Richard Carr Glynn'. There are other items of presentation silver including plates, dishes and wine coolers, but a more personal item is a small silver mug bearing the inscription, believed to be genuine, which says, 'Nelson's Grog Mug, used by him on H.M. Ship Victory'. Grog, of course, was the traditional mixture of rum and water issued daily to the men aboard British warships and regarded by many as the lifeblood of the Navy. There is also another cup, carved from a coconut shell, but with a silver rim and three silver legs, made for Nelson by one of the officers aboard his ship in 1797.

Other items with a close Nelson association include one of his prayer books which bears the inscription 'Horatio Nelson, HMS Agamemnon 1781' while other books of his include The *Royal Kalender* 1787 and Goldsmith's *The Vicar of Wakefield*. On the subject

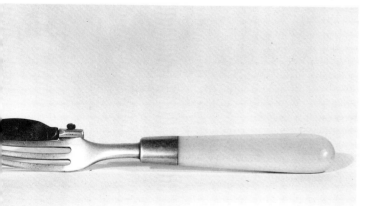

Opposite:
Nelson gave this gold chain with a pendant in the shape of a dog to his daughter Horatia.
National Maritime Museum

Left:
A much admired curiosity is this combined knife and fork used by Nelson after he lost his right arm. Optimised for use with the left hand, examples will be found in several museums.
National Maritime Museum

of books, there is an unusual collection of some of the many biographies of Nelson and descriptions of the Battle of Trafalgar , some wildly inaccurate, that appeared within the two years following Nelson's death. Recalling some of the dangerous incidents in his life is a silver watch bearing an inscription which states that it was 'Presented by Lady Nelson to John Sykes Coxswain for twice saving the life of his commander Sir Horatio Nelson. July 3rd 1797. HMS Theseus'. This of course refers to the incident when Nelson was involved in a hand-to-hand fight aboard his launch off Cadiz in 1797. The other reminder is a shoulder epaulette reputed to be from the uniform which he was wearing when he lost his arm in the assault at Tenerife. One intriguing item is the so-called 'Nelson Cenotaph', a valuable piece commissioned by his friend, Alexander Davison, to commemorate his memory. Unfortunately it was stolen and vandalised many years ago, and when recovered it had been partially broken with some of the more valuable parts missing. The story is told fully later in this chapter.

Several relics of HMS *Victory* are on display along with a fine model of the ship itself. One of these is a small snuff box, with a silver inlay, made out of timber taken from the oak knee which supported Nelson as he lay dying in the cockpit. There are other snuff boxes also made from pieces of the ship's timber and one of these has a representation of the ship behind a glass faced inlay. Another piece of timber is shown in its original state with a French musket ball fired at Trafalgar firmly embedded in it, while other pieces of wood have been used to make models of some of the ship's boats. Most of the wood in the latter examples was taken from the *Victory* while she was undergoing a major restoration between 1925 and 1928.

As with the other museums there is a display of items associated with Nelson's funeral including a silver stave carried at the funeral and inscribed 'Admiral Lord Horatio Nelson, Duke of Brontë, Viscount of the Nile and Burnham Thorpe, KB. Born 1758. Buried with full National Honours at St Paul's Cathedral, 1806'. There is also a full range of commemorative ware including a black basalt Wedgwood teapot, Staffordshire figures, salt glazed stoneware jugs and mugs by Royal Doulton, a Liverpool ware jug and, unusually, a pair of engraved nautilus shells. A collection of commemorative items from the 1905 centenary of Trafalgar complete this display.

Apart from the various items exhibited, the Monmouth museum also houses an extremely important collection of letters, documents, journals and other publications which can be made available for research purposes. Much of the material came from the Llangattock collection of which the most important single item was purchased in 1914. This consisted principally of Nelson's letters to his wife between 1785 until 1800 and is bound in blue leather volumes, one of which contains Lady Nelson's wedding ring in its cover. The other major source of documents came from those

Above:
A silver pocket-watch presented to young Midshipman Nelson after the 1772 Polar expedition. The inscription around the edge reads 'For strict attention to duty with HMS *Racehorse*. North Pole Expedition 1772'. *National Maritime Museum*

Opposite:
The Lloyd's building is one of the most modern in the City of London, but it houses a valuable Nelson collection dating back almost 200 years. *ASM*

originally in the possession of Emma Hamilton and included books of letters, log books, official reports and Nelson's letters to her. Many were sold to raise cash in 1813 and others, which had been passed to her biographer, also came on to the open market shortly afterwards. This resulted in the collection being split up and although some were bought by the family, others disappeared. However, the Monmouth museum has managed to collect a worthwhile cross-section including letter books for 1796 and 1799 through to 1804. There are also Nelson's letters to Lady Hamilton from 1799 through to his death in 1805 and a whole host of unrelated documents from a variety of sources including the papers of his solicitor, William Hazelwood. The whole collection forms a valuable resource for students of Nelson and even now they have not been fully researched.

The other major collection of Nelson material is not, unfortunately, open to the public. The actions of Nelson, and the rest of the Royal Navy, in sweeping the French and Spanish navies from the seas and protecting the interests of British trade around the world, attracted the heartfelt appreciation of the City of London institutions in general and Lloyd's of London in particular. This appreciation was recorded in well publicised ways such as the presentation of money and silver to those who fought in successful engagements, to less well known but still much appreciated gifts and actions to care for the wounded seamen and families of those killed in action. As a frequent recipient of these awards, Nelson became closely connected with Lloyd's, and their chairman, Sir John Julius Angerstein. This association is recorded at Lloyd's by means of a copy of a portrait of Sir John by Sir Thomas Lawrence RA, and copies of correspondence between the two men on the subject of awards to and care of the wounded. After the Battle of the Nile, Lloyd's raised a fund of over £38,000 for such care (a massive sum in those days) and voted £500 for Nelson himself to purchase silver plate. The resulting dinner service was augmented by a similar gift after Copenhagen in 1801 and many pieces from this collection formed the nucleus of a private Nelson museum in Lloyd's modern building in the centre of the City of London. Although a private collection, access by *bona fide* students and researchers can be organised through the Curator.

The display of silver is quite staggering and is all the more interesting as several of the pieces are regularly used by Lloyd's for formal dinners so that not everything here is just a museum exhibit gathering dust. Among the items displayed are a pair of candlesticks (c1743) and bearing the initials 'HN', six soup plates which are of the Copenhagen silver (1801), a small salver with the *San Josef* crest of c1767, a breakfast dish with an engraved inscription on the lid which is believed to have been with Nelson aboard the *Victory* at the time of the Battle of Trafalgar, three rectangular vegetable dishes with lids, the finials of which are decorated in the form of a replica Chelengk (1801), and two oval entrée dishes with lids, also with Chelengk handles (1801). Also on display are some of Nelson's cutlery including a combined knife and fork for a left-handed person, tea caddies and a salver bearing his coat of arms, and a large tray, two large meat dishes, a sauce tureen, wine coolers and a vegetable dish. All of these latter items used today on special occasions. Apart from Nelson's own silver, there is also a display of plate presented to Captain Darby of HMS *Bellerophon* at the Battle of the Nile which includes tureens, teapot and stand, basket dish with handle, stem cups, salver, entrée dishes and presentation cup, all of which is engraved with inscriptions relating to the battle.

Nelson was also generous on his own account and on display here are a number of gifts which he made to friends and colleagues. There is, for example, a cup given to his nephew Nelson Suckling in 1805, a holder in the form of a silver jolly boat containing two decanters presented to Thomas Atkinson in 1801, and a teapot given to one of his captains at the Nile, Thomas Miller, in 1797.

In 1803, when war broke out again following the short-lived Peace of Amiens, Lloyd's resolved to set up a permanent fund to replace the *ad hoc* charitable collections previously made after various actions. Known as the Patriotic Fund, it included subscriptions and contributions made by organisations and individuals throughout the country and, apart from continuing to provide for injured soldiers and sailors and their families, it also instituted the award of silver vases and presentation swords to Army and Navy officers who distinguished themselves in action. The vases were magnificent creations, mostly valued at £100 although some cost up to £500, and there are several examples on display including one awarded to Edward Rotheram who commanded HMS *Royal Sovereign*, Collingwood's flagship at Trafalgar, another to Mrs Sophia Duff, wife of Captain George Duff of HMS *Mars* who was killed during the battle, and one to the Earl of Northesk who was third-in-command at the Battle of Trafalgar aboard HMS *Britannia*. Patriotic Fund swords came in three versions: mates and midshipmen would receive one valued at £30, lieutenants a £50 sword, while captains and flag officers received the ornate £100 sword. After Trafalgar, all the captains who took part in the battle were awarded £100 swords and that presented to Captain R. Grindal of HMS *Prince* is displayed in the collection. There are also several other swords and vases on display awarded for actions unconnected with Nelson or Trafalgar, while some interesting documents recording the formal resolutions of the Patriotic Fund Committee in respect of the award of swords and vases to officers and grants to the wounded and bereaved relatives can also be seen.

The collection also holds a number of letters and documents directly relating to Nelson including the commission appointing Nelson to command of HMS *Hinchingbroke*, his first command as a post captain, which is signed by Admiral Sir Peter Parker, C-in-C West Indies, 26 May 1779. To accompany this is a Good Conduct Certificate signed by the captain of HMS *Lowestoft* (William Locker) when Nelson

Opposite:
A silver candlestick, one of many pieces of silver belonging to Nelson on display at Lloyd's. *ASM*

Left:
This silver salver shows the *San Josef* motif which decorated much of Nelson's silver and porcelain. *ASM*

left the ship in 1778 at Port Royal, Jamaica. There are also a number of letters and orders written by Nelson himself, including a selection chosen to illustrate the changes in his handwriting style due to the loss of his right arm. The first of these is to a Thomas Pollard and is dated 27 June 1794 and headed 'Camp near Calvi', this being just before he lost the sight of his right eye. Another is addressed to Sir John Jervis and dated 15 July 1797, a few days before Nelson lost his arm at Tenerife, and is one of the last letters written with his right hand in a tidy slanting style. The next is dated September 1797 when he had returned to England after the tragedy at Tenerife and is addressed to the Reverend Dixon Hoste at Bath. This is an early example of his left-handed style and is square, jerky and upright, as might be expected. However, another letter, written off Malta on 27 February 1800 and addressed to Mrs William Suckling, shows the more mature left-handed style which he eventually achieved. There are other letters on display as well as examples of his orders including the setting out of flag pendants and signals, shown in colour, issued 10 October 1805 for use at Trafalgar (this would have been drawn up by one of his officers but it bears Nelson's signature). The Lloyd's collection also holds the original log of the frigate HMS *Euryalus* and is shown open at the page which records receipt of Nelson's famous flag signal (a facsimile of this log can be seen at the Bucklers Hard Maritime Museum).

During his lifetime, Nelson was the recipient of numerous orders and decorations of which four were of particular importance and he constantly wore their insignia on his uniform. These were those of a knight of the most honourable Order of the Bath (KB), a knight of the Order of St Ferdinand and of Merit (awarded by the Kingdom of the Two Sicilies), a knight of the Turkish Order of the Crescent (Ottoman Empire) and a knight of the Chapteral Order of St Joachim (German States). The cloth and gilt insignia of these orders can be seen sewn on Nelson's uniforms displayed at other museums, but unique to the Lloyd's collection is his Order of the Bath, complete with gold chain and original insignia. This was conferred following the Battle of St Vincent. Traditionally the insignia of such orders are returned to the sovereign on the death of the recipient, but this is one of only two such orders in private hands, the other being that of Nelson's illustrious contemporary, the Duke of Wellington. The collection also holds examples of the insignia of his other orders as well as a collection of various medals issued to commemorate his battles and the occasion of his state funeral. An unusual exhibit is a pewter medal presented to Royal Marines who formed the guard of honour at the official unveiling of Nelson's Column in Trafalgar Square in 1844. As might be expected, there is also a display relating to the funeral, but this mostly contains items similar to those in other establishments except for a gold pendant containing a lock of Nelson's hair and which belonged to Emma Hamilton.

A more unusual display contains material relating to Nelson's flag captain, Hardy, who later rose to become an Admiral and there is a print portraying him in the uniform of that rank. Other items include a letter written by Hardy when a Vice-Admiral in October 1831 and a sword presented to him and bearing an inscription relating to his valour at the Battle of Trafalgar. An intriguing object is a walking cane with miniature telescope set into the handle and this was actually presented to Captain Hardy by Nelson in 1798.

Finally there is a painting of Nelson by Lemuel Abbott completed in 1798. Dominating the centre of the display area, it is an unusual work by the artist in that it is a full length portrait, Abbott being better known for his numerous head and shoulder likenesses of Nelson. The painting shows signs of having been altered after completion in order to show the orders and medals awarded after the Battle of the Nile which occurred in August of that year. Overall, the Lloyd's Nelson collection is one of the most fascinating to be seen and it is unfortunate that it is not open to the general public. Of course, the value of some of the items is incalculable and consequently the security arrangements are probably the equal of those surrounding the crown jewels! However, the curator of the collection will treat any requests to view the collection sympathetically and can be contacted through Lloyd's of London.

Apart from the major collections already described, the best place to find reminders and remnants of Nelson is in his home county of Norfolk where several museums have items of interest. The most accessible is probably the Castle Museum at Norwich which houses various collections of local interest. On the first floor, overlooking the entrance gallery, is a display of Nelsonia which includes a few personal objects including the very hat he wore when sitting for a portrait painted for the City of Norwich in 1801 by Sir William Beechey and which now hangs in the city's Blackfriars Hall. There is also a penknife and its wooden sheath which belonged to Nelson when he was a boy but the rest of the display consists mostly of items which can also be seen in other places, such as various medals, a mourning ring, and some commemorative ware. The latter includes a Staffordshire group of figures portraying the Death of Nelson, made in 1845 when there was a revival of interest in such commemorative pieces due to the publicity surrounding the completion of Nelson's Column in Trafalgar Square that year. Elsewhere in the Castle Museum can be found a green painted chair reputed to have come from HMS *Victory* and a bronze bust of Nelson by Peter Turnerelli.

Out and about in Norfolk, the museum at King's Lynn has a fine model of Nelson's funeral barge and a Lemuel Abbott portrait, while the Yarmouth Maritime Museum has a piece of the drape which covered the funeral car during the procession to St Paul's. Yarmouth normally has a small display of prints and facsimiles to demonstrate the town's connection with Nelson and, at the time of writing, has commissioned an accurate replica of his uniform based on one displayed at Greenwich. This museum also possesses an excellent library which contains many books of value to students of Nelson including a complete run of the Naval Chronicle which was published from 1799 to 1819 and contains many references to the man. The most significant, in Volume III, is a *Sketch of His Life* written for the publication by Nelson himself. Other works include Campbell's *Lives of the Admirals* and A Life of Nelson by the great American naval historian, Admiral A. T. Mahan. Absolutely invaluable is a full set (7 Vols) of *The Dispatches and Letters of Vice Admiral Lord Viscount Nelson* collected and edited by Sir Harris Nicolas between 1844 and 1846. These have been referred to as the 'Bible of the Nelson student' and serve as an illustration of the great wealth of material available to historians today.

In this catalogue of what is left of Nelson, it is perhaps appropriate to return to his birthplace at Burnham Thorpe where, in the possession of the parish of All Saints' is Nelson's wooden medicine chest. Like many pieces designed for travelling and use at sea, this is of an ingenious design with several compartments and drawers to hold a selection of bottles, phials, pill boxes and powders. The church also owns a glass goblet which was

Above:
A chair on display at the Castle Museum, Norwich, is believed to have come from a set used aboard the *Victory*. *ASM, by permission of the Curator*

presented to Nelson by the City of Norwich after the Battle of the Nile and carries the inscription 'Admiral Nelson Glorious'. These items are not normally displayed in public but can sometimes be seen by arrangement with the rector.

Of course these are not the only pieces not to be seen in public. There are many private collections, large and small, containing all sorts of objects connected with Nelson. Many of these are in the possession of his descendants but there are also private individuals who have built up their own valuable collections over the years. Occasionally a letter, document or artefact will come up for auction and fetch a high price, even though the authenticity of such items may be in doubt. In view of the great value (even a single letter can be sold for several thousands of pounds) attached to anything connected with Nelson, private collectors are naturally reticent about letting details of their possessions become known in case they become a target for burglary or theft and consequently the existence of many items of great interest will remain known only to a small circle of collectors and historians. However, it is possible for people of quite modest means to join in and build up their own collections of Nelsonia at more down to earth prices, although they would be most unlikely to obtain anything which actually belonged to Nelson. However, items such as contemporary prints can be picked up quite cheaply and some interesting commemorative pieces will sometimes be spotted. For example, some of the prints reproduced in this book were obtained for less than £10 each, while a 1930s metal biscuit tin bearing a portrait of Emma Hamilton was seen in an antique shop for only £12. So the potential is there! You may not be able to emulate the great collectors such as Lady Llangattock or Mrs Lambert McCarthy but you can share the enjoyment of rooting around in markets, fairs, auctions and antique shops and in the excitement of turning up something having a connection, no matter how remote, with Nelson himself and the era when Britannia truly ruled the waves.

Forgeries and Thefts

From the time of his death in 1805, anything connected with Nelson has been avidly sought by collectors many of whom merely look for some tangible reminder of their admiration for the man and his eventful life. Others may, quite legitimately, acquire documents, personal possessions and ephemera as an investment, knowing that a ready market exists for any item with a genuine Nelson connection. However, the demand by collectors for what is, after all, a finite quantity of material has led several unscrupulous people to offer an item for sale for which the alleged connection with Nelson is at best unproven or, at worst, completely falsified. In recent years, for example, an auction house offered a letter for sale, representing that it bore the signature of Nelson even though several experts stated categorically that it was not the great man's hand that had penned the signature. Eventually it was withdrawn, but only after considerable adverse publicity.

Such events are not new and one of the fascinating aspects of a visit to the Nelson Museum at Monmouth is a collection of various items which were purported to have belonged to Nelson, or to have been associated with him, but which are fakes of one sort or another. Perhaps the most obvious is Nelson's false eye! Many representations of Nelson show him with a patch over one eye, pirate style, although he never in fact wore such a patch and nor did he actually lose his eye (his injuries in Corsica were such as to cost him the sight of his right eye but it was not removed). The eye shown at Monmouth is in fact a model of the type commonly used during the 19th century to instruct medical students and how it came to be in the Llangattock collection is not known. She must have realised that it was not a genuine artefact, but was perhaps amused at the idea of having Nelson's 'glass eye'.

One common method of trapping the unwary purchaser was to take any piece of silver, or other appropriate item, and have it engraved with the letters 'HN' or some other inscription. In some cases it would then be difficult to prove that the particular item did NOT belong to Nelson. However, unscrupulous vendors did not always disguise their work very thoroughly as shown by several exhibits at Monmouth. There is a dress sword bearing an inscription to Nelson and carrying his crest and coronet. Unfortunately the sword was not manufactured until 1854, almost 50 years after Trafalgar. In the same category is a midshipman's sword with an aged label stating that it was used by Nelson although in this case the sword is of a pattern which was not introduced until 1825. A similar forgery is a silver gilt compass bearing an inscription stating that it was presented to Nelson by Emma Hamilton in July 1798 but, apart from the fact that such a gift was unlikely to have been made at that time, it was actually made by a craftsman named Dolland in 1820.

Inscribed silverware is a common trap for the unwary and examples on show include a silver cup with a boxed knife, fork and spoon set bearing the inscription 'Bought by Nelson, August 1805, for Horatia', although the items are variously hallmarked in the period 1805 to 1808. A more subtle forgery is a pair of silver jugs made in 1767 and 1789 respectively and inscribed as being a gift from 'Admirers' in 1802. The clue here is that the style of the inscription is of a period recognisably later than 1802. Sometimes forgers are caught out by their own ignorance of the facts as in a boxed set of steel cutlery which bears a plaque stating that it was presented to Viscount Nelson by the Birmingham Society of Steelmakers on 4 September 1792. Unfortunately, Nelson was not created a Viscount until 1801, following the Battle of Copenhagen. Even the National Maritime Museum at Greenwich can show similar examples, such as a chased silver goblet bearing an inscription dated 1799 although the piece was actually made in Dublin in 1807! Also at Greenwich are examples of porcelain forgeries such as a teacup and saucer made in Paris and a Chinese plate, both decorated in the manner of Nelson's own pieces but with incorrect or misspelt mottoes.

One commonly seen forgery is a purported edition of *The Times* newspaper dated 7 November 1805 and bearing news of the Battle of Trafalgar. There are several false versions of this in circulation but in some cases they can immediately be recognised as such. Some are so crude as to have the wrong date printed while genuine editions of *The Times* at that period had the front page given over to classified advertisements with even the most important news being relegated to the inside pages, a point often forgotten by would-be forgers. There are also a number of other items on display at Monmouth where it is not possible to prove one way or the other whether they ever belonged to Nelson and examples include a brass telescope inscribed 'Horatio Nelson, the gift of his affectionate Father', and a combined compass and sundial merely marked 'HN'. While there is no reason to think that these are forgeries, by the same token it is impossible at this stage to conclusively prove that they *did* belong to Nelson.

Although the Monmouth Museum display illustrates the variety of forgeries which have been perpetrated, it also has first-hand experience of another major problem to beset owners of valuable Nelson memorabilia — theft. After Nelson's death, a purse containing 84 golden guineas was found in his cabin. These subsequently came into the possession of his friend and prize agent, Alexander Davison, who had them mounted on a gold pyramid, 21 of the coins on each face, and the whole mounted on an ornate base and supported by four gilded cast figures of Fame. In the centre of the base, under the shade of the pyramid was a plinth bearing a sarcophagus surmounted by a cushion and coronet. Handles on the sarcophagus were in the representation of the bow and stern of the barge used to carry Nelson's body up the Thames on the occasion of his funeral. The whole assembly was known as the Nelson Cenotaph and it had a chequered history, passing through the hands of various collectors until ending up in the Llangattock collection at Monmouth. A television programme in 1953 commemorating the Battle of

Trafalgar, during which the Cenotaph and other items in the museum were featured, obviously prompted a robbery which occurred shortly afterwards. No less than 91 exhibits were stolen including the 84 guineas which were broken off from the Cenotaph. A few months later the police tracked down and arrested the thief, recovering some 60 of the stolen items. However, the guineas had been sold for only £100 and were never located, it being thought likely that they had been melted down for the gold value. The Cenotaph is still on display at Monmouth, but now lacks the pyramid and Nelson's coins.

Almost all paintings and other representations of Nelson show his two Naval Gold Medals, awarded for his part in the Battle of St Vincent and also the Battle of the Nile. These medals were kept by his descendants and after being exhibited at the Royal Navy Exhibition, Chelsea, in 1891 they were subsequently loaned by Viscount Bridport to the Greenwich Hospital Museum where they were displayed in the Painted Hall along with other possessions including his uniforms. The medals were stolen on the night of 8 December 1900, and they have not been seen since.

Even in modern times, when it might be thought that the value of Nelson items is recognised and security precautions are much stricter, spectacular thefts still occur. In October 1993 a valuable gilt framed portrait of Nelson by Hoppner was found to be

missing from the Maritime Museum at Great Yarmouth. This has not been recovered, nor has another portrait by Sir William Beechey which was stolen from the Norfolk Club, Norwich, the previous year. In view of the special nature of the paintings, it seems likely that they were stolen 'to order' at the behest of unscrupulous collectors. As a consequence of this sort of activity, most museums have considerably tightened their security and in some cases important exhibits have been replaced by replicas or facsimiles.

Left:
The 'glass eye' on display at the Nelson Museum, Monmouth, is one of the better known fake artifacts associated with Nelson. *Nelson Museum, Monmouth*

4: NELSON'S SHIPS
AND HIS NAVY

Although there is much to see on land and in museums connected with Nelson and his life, it was at sea that he won the reputation and honours that made him a national hero and it was at sea that he lost his life in the service of his country. We are, therefore, very fortunate in that it is still possible to gain a real insight into the way that he would have lived and fought by visiting his actual flagship at the Battle of Trafalgar — HMS *Victory*. A tour around the ship to see the crowded messdecks, the rows of cannon on the gundecks, the officers' cabins, the complexity of the rigging and masts, the solid timbers of the ship's frame and the darkened cockpit where Nelson died will leave an indelible impression and a sense of wonder that men could live and fight in such a confined environment. In order to appreciate fully the spectacle of HMS *Victory*, it will be useful to understand the organisation and manning of the Royal Navy during Nelson's time and to review the history of the wooden fighting ship up to the time of Trafalgar when its efficiency as a weapon of war was virtually at its peak.

It is King Henry VIII who is generally considered to be the father of what might be regarded as the conventional cannon-armed sailing man-of-war. During the 15th century the cannon had revolutionised land warfare and already attempts had been made to mount these weapons on ships. Henry's great step forward was to have his ships designed with a continuous gundeck so that more and heavier guns could be carried, and one of the first, the *Mary Rose*, can still be seen today at Portsmouth, not far from Nelson's *Victory*. Built in 1509-10, the *Mary Rose* was subsequently rebuilt and rearmed in 1536 but then sank while sailing out of Portsmouth to engage a French fleet off

Spithead in 1545 due to water entering the open gunports as she heeled in the wind. The wreck lay undisturbed for centuries before being recovered onshore in 1982 and was subsequently housed in the building which serves as the *Mary Rose* museum today.

During the century following the building of the *Mary Rose*, the sailing warship grew in size and power and in 1610 the world's first three-decker, the *Prince Royal*, was floated out of her building dock at Woolwich. By later standards she was lightly armed, carrying 55 guns, but she was the most powerful ship of her time and the trend was continued with the magnificent *Sovereign of the Seas* (1637) built for the Navy under Charles I. Also a three-decker, she carried over 100 guns on three flush gundecks, and compared to earlier ships she carried additional sails in the form of topgallant sails on her fore and mizzen masts and a royal sail on the main, and in this she was well ahead of her time. Her hull had a total length of 234ft while the main gundeck was over 167ft long. Renamed *Royal Sovereign* in 1660, she had a long career until accidently destroyed by fire in 1696 but in many respects she was the true prototype of the ship-of-the-line which, except in detail, remained almost unchanged for the next 200 years.

During the time of Charles I there was also another major step forward in the history of the fighting ship. Until that time each ship was built as a 'one-off' and consequently no two ships were the same in respect of size, armament, crew or sailing qualities. However, during the 1620s 10 small 14-gun warships were built to protect merchant ships from the depredations of privateers in the English Channel. These were named as the *First* to *Tenth Whelp* and were the first example of a class of warships being built to a standard design. Another concept aimed at some form of standardisation was the idea of rating ships according to some measurable criteria. Initially this was based on the number of men required to man the guns but later this was changed and was based solely on the number of guns carried, although this in turn was in accordance with various official 'Establishments' which were revised at intervals and laid down strict parameters for each class of ship including the dimensions of hulls and fittings, masts and spars, thicknesses of various timbers to be used, and size and composition of armament.

In the mid-18th century, a number of changes and reforms in warship design were introduced under the direction of Admiral Anson in conjunction with his Surveyor of the Navy, Sir Thomas Slade, a master shipwright who was also the designer of HMS *Victory*. By Nelson's time, ships-of-the-line and frigates were rated according to the number of guns which they mounted, ranging from the three-decker First Rates mounting over 100 guns down to a Sixth Rate frigate carrying roughly two dozen guns. The armament a ship carried gave an instant impression of its size and power, and consequently it was accepted practice that the name of the ship was invariably followed by the number of guns it mounted. Thus, for example, one would see written *Neptune 98, Swiftsure 74*, or *Euryalus 36*. In action the vast majority of the crew were engaged in serving the guns and consequently the ship's complement was to a large extent determined by the number of guns, as illustrated by this table which lists the official number of guns carried by each of the Rates, together with an indication of the likely size of the crew:

First Rate	Over 100 guns	900-850 men
Second Rate	90-98 guns	750 men
Third Rate	64-80 guns	390-720 men
Fourth Rate	50 guns	350 men
Fifth Rate	32-44 guns	250-320 men
Sixth Rate	24-28 guns	200-250 men

Opposite:
HMS *Victory*, Nelson's flagship at Trafalgar, is magnificently preserved at Portsmouth and is open for public viewing.
ASM

Of these ships, only the Fourth Rate and above were regarded as fit to lie in the line of battle and the smaller ships were more often referred to under the general classification of frigates. In addition there were even smaller types of vessel such as brigs and cutters but these were generally used as dispatch vessels and occasionally for inshore actions.

Amongst the larger ships, the differences were not confined solely to the number of guns. The First and Second Rates always had three gundecks and were normally allocated as flagships to commanders of fleets and squadrons, their greater size providing more room for the senior officer and his staff. Although the term Third Rate covered ships of varying size, by the time of the Napoleonic wars of the late 18th century the Royal Navy had standardised on a type of ship which had good sailing qualities and mounted 74 guns on two gundecks, Indeed, an examination of the composition of the fleets at the Battles of the Nile, Copenhagen and Trafalgar will show that the overwhelming majority of these ships were 74s. During the early part of the 18th century the three-decked 80-gun ship was regarded as the standard for a Third Rate but experience showed that they could be unwieldy to handle and on occasions the gunports on the lower deck where the heaviest guns were mounted could not be opened because they were too close to the water as the ship heeled in the wind. The 74 was evolved as a more balanced design carrying its guns on two decks so that the lower gundeck was much higher out of the water and was less likely to be affected by sailing conditions. As was often the case at that time, changes in the design of British ships came about as a result of observing and using captured French and Spanish ships. Although it is debatable whether the French actually invented the 74, they certainly were quick to adopt it and the Royal Navy rapidly followed suit. By the time of the Napoleonic Wars, the 74 was established as the principal component of the British fleet and indeed the mere mention of the words 'Seventy Four' were enough to conjure up images of British seapower and a string of successful battles in the mind of the ordinary Englishman.

Similarly it was the French who first built what was to become the well-known frigate of Nelson's time. Previously tasks such as escorting convoys, fighting minor actions and scouting were carried out by Sixth Rates or smaller two-decked ships but the concept of a fast sailing ship mounting around 30-36 guns on a single gundeck came from the French. The space saved on the lower deck could then be used for stowing additional stores, making these ships suitable for wide-ranging detachments away from the main fleet — a very useful attribute to the Royal Navy with its worldwide commitments. In general the fast sailing frigates would be dispatched by an Admiral to seek out the enemy and report his whereabouts so that the main fleet could be brought up and, hopefully, a successful battle be fought. However, this theory did not always work and on occasions the lightly-armed frigates would find themselves in action against much larger ships and some very famous actions were fought in such circumstances where some of the most stirring tales of bravery and heroism in the Navy's history can be found.

The number of guns carried was not the only factor to determine the relative strength of an individual warship as in general the larger ships could also carry heavier guns, considerably increasing the weight of the broadside. Guns were categorised by the weight of the roundshot which they fired and Nelson's ships generally carried 6, 9, 12, 18, 24 or 32 pounders in various combinations. During most of the 18th century, a number of First Rate ships had carried 42-pounders on their main gundeck but by the time of Trafalgar all such ships had been rearmed with the lighter and faster firing 32-pounder. First and Second Rates carried the heaviest guns on the main gundeck only, lighter pieces being carried on the upper decks. A typical example is HMS *Foudroyant 80* which served as Nelson's flagship for a time in the Mediterranean. Completed in 1798, she was armed with 30 32-pounders on the gundeck, 32 24-pounders on the upper deck and a total of 18 12-pounders on the forecastle and quarterdeck. A typical 74, such as HMS *Mars* which fought at Trafalgar, was armed with 28 32-pounders, 30 24-pounders and 16 9-pounders. HMS *Phoebe* (launched 1795) was typical of many of Nelson's frigates with an armament of 26 18-pounders on the gundeck, eight nine-pounders on the quarterdeck and a further two nine-pounders on the forecastle for use as bowchasers. In addition to the normal guns, from around 1780 most ships also carried an additional weapon known as a carronade, named after the Carron Iron Co at Falkirk where they were invented. These guns had a shorter barrel than a standard cannon, and used a reduced charge to fire similar sized shots. The theory behind this was that, at short ranges, the shot would cause more impact damage than one fired at high velocity

Opposite:
A fascinating sectional model of HMS *Illustrious*, a typical 74, built at Bucklers Hard and launched in 1789. At the bottom of the hull is the hold containing stores and magazines, above that is the orlop deck mostly taken up with accommodation for seamen and warrant officers, next come the two gundecks surmounted by the quarterdeck at the stern incorporating the captain's suite of cabins. *ASM, by permission of the Curator, Bucklers Hard*

Above:
HMS *Euryalus*, a 36-gun frigate present at Trafalgar. *ASM, by permission of the Curator, Bucklers Hard*

which might well pass right through an enemy ship. As they were much lighter and had less recoil than conventional cannons, they were generally carried on slide mountings, sited on the quarterdeck and forecastle of larger ships, and often formed a significant proportion of the armament of smaller ships such as frigates. Confusingly they were not normally included in the number of guns which determined the ship's rate. Thus a 36-gun frigate might carry as many as 42 guns if the carronades were included. At Trafalgar, the *Victory* carried two 68-pounder carronades mounted on the forecastle and in fact it was one of these which fired her opening shot of the battle, into the stern of the French *Bucentaure*.

All of these weapons were simple muzzle-loaders but to achieve high rates of fire and well-timed broadsides was a complex routine demanding a very high level of skill, training and discipline, and it was in these qualities that the Royal Navy outclassed its opponents. A 32-pounder actually weighed 59cwt (or 2,997kg) and was mounted on a wheeled wooden gun carriage which was controlled by means of ropes and lines. The gun crew consisted of 13 men under a gun captain and each man was assigned precise and specific duties to carry out in the process of loading, running up and firing the gun. In Nelson's time the drill had been reduced to 14 precise orders which covered every necessary action and ship's captains would constantly exercise their gun crews so that they would be able to carry on firing efficiently in the heat and din of battle even if some of their number should be killed or wounded.

When the enemy was sighted, the captain would order the ship to be 'cleared for action'. While at sea the guns were normally firmly lashed down so that they could not move about as the ship pitched and rolled under the motion of the waves. A loose cannon was a dangerous animal and more than one ship had been lost because a heavy cannon broke loose in rough seas and either caused the ship to capsize due to the sudden transfer of weight or else holed the ship's hull due to the impact of three tons of iron smashing through the fragile timbers. However, with action approaching, the guns

were unlashed but still restrained by the controlling block and tackle on each side. The barrel was levelled and the muzzle plug (tompion) removed. It was quite usual for guns to be kept loaded with powder and ball so that they would be ready at any time for instant action and, if this was the case, the gunports could be opened and the guns run out by hauling on the side and quarter tackles. The charge of gunpowder was held in a flannel cartridge and so the next action was to press a quill or needle though a small hole (vent) in the breech of the gun in order to prick the cartridge bag. Firing was effected by pulling a lanyard attached to a flintlock mechanism mounted over the vent and this had to be primed by depositing a small amount of powder in the mechanism's pan. When the lanyard was pulled, the flint striker sprung forward creating a shower of sparks which ignited the powder in the pan. The heat of this ignition travelled down the vent, through the hole previously pricked in the cartridge bag and set off the main charge. As the gun fired it would recoil with tremendous force, restrained only by the thick breech rope which was fed through a ring on the rear face (cascabel) of the cannon. It will be appreciated that it was essential for all members of the gun crew to be standing well clear at the time of firing, but this was easier said than done in the confined space of a ship's gundeck. Think about it as you stand in the low-vaulted gundecks of HMS *Victory* and try to picture the scene as the guns recoil, accompanied by clouds of dense acrid smoke blown in through the gunport, gun captains scream orders as they try and make themselves heard above the ear shattering detonations of the cannons, the cries and yells of the wounded forming an aural backdrop, and all the time the routine being interrupted by the crash of enemy shot hitting the ship and sending shards of lethal timber flying around.

As soon as the gun was fired, the crew would leap upon it, two men sponging out the barrel with a moist sponge to extinguish any remaining burning material which could otherwise cause a premature ignition of the next cartridge to be loaded. The new

Opposite:
A 32-pounder gun of the type carried in the lower gundeck of First Rates including HMS *Victory*. *ASM*

Above:
24-pounder guns on the middle gundeck of HMS *Victory*. The headroom on the gundecks was around 5ft, the minimum height necessary to work the guns. *ASM*

cartridge was then brought up to the muzzle and rammed down the barrel, to be followed by a cloth wad and then the iron roundshot, then a further wad, each one rammed home. The iron shot were not designed to be a tight fit in the barrel as this would slow down the loading cycle but this also meant that there was a slight gap (known as windage) between the shot and the barrel sides. This reduced the efficiency of the gun as the explosive gases could thus leak out, causing a loss of range and accuracy. It was in an attempt to reduce this effect that the cloth wads were rammed down before and after the shot. As soon as the gun was loaded, it was hauled forward using the side tackle, and primed ready for firing.

In most actions, after the initial broadside, the guns were reloaded and fired individually so that after the first two or three rounds, the firing was almost continuous along the side of the ship as each gun was fired as soon as it was ready. Even the initial broadside did not comprise firing all the guns simultaneously as the resulting recoil would place too much of a strain on the ship's structure. Instead they would be fired in batteries of, say, four or eight guns, with a very slight pause between each battery firing. Alternatively they might be fired one at a time as each gun came to bear on the target.

When clearing a ship for action, it was not just a question of preparing and running out the guns. There were many other essential tasks to be done so that the ship would be in a fit state to fight its own weapons, accept damage from enemy fire and look after its own casualties. Many of the officers' cabins, including those of the captain and admiral situated below the quarterdeck, also formed part of the gundecks and housed guns. These cabins had to be stripped and the officers' luggage and possessions struck down to the ship's hold. The bulkheads between the cabins were often removable and these would also be taken down and stowed. On deck, nets would be rigged to prevent boarders leaping across from another ship, and hammocks would be stowed along the top of the bulwarks to provide additional protection from musket fire and splinters. Unless engaged in a chase, many of the upper sails and spars would be lowered and brought down to the deck so that they would be not be carried away during the action. The ship's boats would be swung overboard and towed astern where they were less likely to be damaged and would also be instantly available if required. Below, the gundecks would be sanded to make them less slippery, a potential problem when the blood literally began to flow from seriously wounded sailors. Finally,

Above opposite:
A replica 68-pounder carronade mounted on the *Victory*'s forecastle. These were lightweight weapons intended for close range action and were usually mounted on slides, as shown here, rather than the wheeled gun carriage of the heavier long barrelled cannons. *ASM*

Opposite:
A variety of ship's cannon on display at Chatham Historic Dockyard. On the rack in the background can be seen some of the implements used in the loading of the guns. *ASM*

Above:
A model of a typical ship-of-the-line showing how the ship's boats were stowed over the waist. In action these boats would be hoisted out and towed astern. *ASM, by permission of the Curator, Bucklers Hard*

deep down in the orlop or cockpit, the surgeon would lay out his instruments and prepare tables to use for operating on wounded sailors. In the meantime the guns would be manned as all the other tasks were completed, the battery officers ready to relay orders by means of speaking trumpets, the powder monkeys (usually young boys) ready with their cartridge cases, and the captain and executive officers on the quarterdeck anxiously watching the enemy. Despite the tasks to be done, a well-drilled ship could clear for action in well under 10min but there then usually followed a long period of anticipation while the opposing forces came closer together and action commenced. This period could often last several hours, especially if the wind was light and the ships were moving only slowly, and it was essential to maintain morale. Men would pray and even make wills (Nelson did both at Trafalgar) while the captain might order a musician or even the marine band to play. It was partly to entertain his men that Nelson made his famous signal as the fleets slowly closed at the Battle of Trafalgar.

What kind of men were to be found aboard a sailing warship of Nelson's navy? Briefly they can be divided into three distinct categories. First and foremost were the commissioned officers who commanded and directed the ships. At that time a naval career was regarded as a very honourable profession and even members of the Royal Family had served as officers and captains — a tradition which continues today. Other officers would come from the ranks of the aristocracy but most of them, including Nelson himself, were the sons of middle-class families who had received at least a good basic education. A boy's naval career could start at a very young age; Nelson was only just 12 years old when he went to sea and this was by no means unusual. A first appointment depended to a large extent on patronage (who you knew) and captains had enormous personal latitude in deciding who was appointed to their ship. On being given command of a ship, particularly one newly-commissioned, his first task would be to find enough men to man her. The Admiralty might well appoint many of the officers and draft in a proportion of the crew, but the rest was up to him. There would be no shortage of friends and relations with young sons to place in the world and many of these would find themselves cold and homesick aboard a fighting man-of-war as a 'captain's servant' while a small proportion would be appointed from the few Naval academies which existed. However the potential young officers were recruited, they were normally appointed as midshipmen from around the age of 15 years and would then serve as ship's officers while at the same time learning all aspects of the naval profession including seamanship, navigation and gunnery. Normally promotion to the rank of lieutenant could occur after serving six years at sea as a midshipman, subject to satisfactory reports and passing an examination board. Whilst exceptionally well connected young men might be able to circumvent some of the requirements, the majority earned their promotion in this way and on the whole the Navy compared favourably with the Army where commissions up to quite senior level could be bought by anybody with the necessary funds at their disposal.

Once promoted, the officer would then be appointed to a ship where he would become the junior amongst five or six lieutenants aboard a ship-of-the-line, or fewer on a frigate or smaller ship. Seniority, based on the date of promotion was all-important. If a lieutenant was posted to a new ship, his ranking amongst the other lieutenants would be determined by their relative dates of appointment to the rank. Eventually he might rise, by dint of effort and good fortune, to become the First Lieutenant, responsible to the captain for the efficient organisation of the ship and the administration of its day-to-day routine. Some lieutenants might be fortunate enough to be given command of a small ship, such as a sloop or a brig, which was not of an established rate to require the appointment of a Post Captain. In such cases the officer was termed as master and commander but this was a position, not a rank, and on completion of the commission the officer might well revert to being a lieutenant.

The all-important step in promotion, the one desired by all naval officers and, at the same time, the most difficult to achieve, was to be made Post. When this happened, the lieutenant was appointed to the Post of Captain which was a substantive rank and his name was entered at the bottom of the Captain's section of the Navy List. From this point on it was merely a question of time, waiting for all the Post Captains senior to him to be promoted or die, until our officer was himself promoted to the rank of Admiral and able to hoist his distinguishing flag at sea. Promotion to Post Captain was achieved basically in two ways: either by routine appointments which usually went to the protégés of various Admirals or other influential people, or as a result of participating in a successful action. Thus for example, all the First Lieutenants aboard Nelson's ships at the Battle of the Nile were promoted to Post Captain as part of the awards meted out for this famous victory.

As a captain, date of seniority was still all-important since, as well as determining when further promotion was due, it also determined who commanded a group of ships when no admiral was present. In such circumstances the senior captain took command and if such a group was actually formed on official instructions from a Commander-in-Chief then he would act as commodore and hoist a broad pennant at his masthead to denote his position. Again, commodore was a position and not a rank as it is today. In the 17th century it had been the practice to divide large fleets into three squadrons each commanded by an Admiral who flew a distinguishing white, blue or red ensign according to seniority. By Nelson's time this system was not strictly adhered to but on promotion from Captain an officer

Opposite:
This dramatic scene shows the conditions that existed on board HMS *Victory* during the Battle of Trafalgar. it is taken from a lithograph by the artist W. H. Overend Entitled 'The Hero of Trafalgar'. *Nelson Museum, Monmouth*

became a Rear-Admiral of the Blue, and subsequently Rear-Admiral of the White and then of the Red. Thereafter further promotion, again according to seniority, proceeded through the three stages of a Vice-Admiral to becoming a full Admiral, again with the flag colours distinguishing seniority. It should be noted that promotion to Captain or Admiral did not necessarily lead to an appointment to command a ship or a fleet. In time of peace officers were laid off on half pay and even in time of war there might not be enough ships to provide jobs for every captain on the List. Amongst admirals there was even less chance of employment as Flag posts were necessarily limited by their very nature.

Nelson's own career neatly illustrates the sort of progression that might be attained, although his subsequent career rested partly on the fact that, through a combination of patronage and ability, he achieved very early promotion to Captain. Even so, he was not guaranteed a job for life and, along with many others, spent five frustrating years ashore on half pay. Even as an admiral, he constantly worried in case he should not be employed, especially after losing his arm at Santa Cruz although, fortunately for Great Britain, in the event his talents were amply utilised. The following table lists Nelson's naval career and can, at least in its early stages, be regarded as typical of the period for a competent officer with some patronage available to him.

NELSON'S NAVAL CAREER

Date	Rank	Notes
1771	Captain's Servant /Midshipman	Joined Navy aged 12 years
1776	Acting Lieutenant	HMS *Worcester* 64
1777	Lieutenant	Appointed 2nd Lieutenant HMS *Lowestoft* 32
1778	Commander	Brig *Badger*
1779	Post Captain	HMS *Hinchingbroke* 28. Aged 20
1797	Rear-Admiral of the Blue Aged 38	
1799	Rear-Admiral of the Red	
1801	Vice-Admiral of the Blue	
1804	Vice-Admiral of the White	

Apart from the commissioned officers, there were another group of officers who held warrants rather than the Sovereign's commission and these were known, naturally enough, as Warrant Officers. These highly-skilled men were the technical experts or professional sailors whose job was to oversee and perform the technical tasks necessary in the running and maintenance of the ship. Generally there were the Sailing Master, the Boatswain (or Bos'n), the Gunner, the Carpenter and the Purser. Although their duties are mostly self-evident, it is worth pointing out that the Bos'n was responsible for the maintenance and operation of the ship's boats, the rigging and sails, and anchors and cables. Each of these men would be served by Petty Officers known as Mates. Thus, for example, there would be Gunners' Mates and Masters' Mates. These men were almost always volunteers and were generally appointed to a specific ship, often staying with it for the whole of their naval career.

Finally there were the seamen who formed the bulk of the crew and these would come from a variety of sources. A few were professional sailors who had volunteered to join the Royal Navy despite the hardships experienced at sea, although it has to be said that in many cases life ashore was even worse at the time. However, volunteers normally only accounted for around one fifth of a ship's complement and the remainder were either 'quota' men or victims of the notorious press gang. Under the Quota Act, various towns and counties within the United Kingdom were obliged to provide a set number of men for naval service, an early form of national service or conscription. Unfortunately local officials often contrived to meet their quota by emptying the local gaols, workhouses, orphanages and even lunatic asylums. On the other hand the press gang, although it took men against their will, at least operated generally in seaports and consequently often produced trained sailors, or at least men familiar with the sea.

Once this disparate mixture was aboard ship, they were virtually prisoners with little chance of going ashore until the ship decommissioned, and even then they were often transferred directly to another ship. The task of training these men to become useful sailors fell to the Warrant Officers and their mates, while the necessary rigid discipline was enforced by the ship's Master-at-Arms, a Petty Officer who reported directly to the First Lieutenant. Much has been written about the undoubtedly harsh discipline and punishments which were a normal feature of the 18th century Navy, but such accounts must be set against the general background of the times when human life was generally cheaply held and privations and starvation were by no means uncommon ashore. Undoubtedly there were sadists on some ships who could make the men's lives a living hell, but a lot depended on the character of the captain, many of whom were educated men with the best interests of their men at heart. In the final analysis, the Navy would not have achieved so much and be held in such fond regard by the nation if it was all gained solely through the use of a cat o'nine tails.

Finally there is a fourth element of a ship's crew to be considered. Almost all ships from a frigate upwards carried a detachment of Royal Marines and on a First Rate this would consist of as many as 150 men. Even in Nelson's time they were something of an élite corps and were all volunteers with a reputation for unswerving loyalty. As such they were a captain's insurance against any problems with disorderly elements in the rest of the crew and provided sentries at all important locations in the ship such as magazines, store cabins, the captain's quarters and various stairways. A large marine detachment would be commanded by a captain (RM), supported by three lieutenants (RM) and a number of sergeants and corporals. In action they provided a musketry force to sweep the upper deck of an enemy ship and, combined with detachments from other ships, they could form a landing force in amphibious operations.

In a First Rate, such as HMS *Victory*, the total complement was probably around 850 men who had to live, sleep, eat and fight in a ship only 226ft long with a maximum beam of less than 52ft. The seamen mostly lived in the lower gundeck, sleeping in hammocks slung from the deckhead and eating, resting and talking around tables slung between the massive guns. Due to the ever-present danger of fire aboard a wooden ship, there

was only one galley for cooking and boiling water, and this was situated on the middle gundeck. The galley fire was lit only at certain times and extinguished after meals had been prepared. Each group of men, termed a Mess, would pool its allotted ration of food and designate one man as cook who would take it to the galley and prepare a hot meal (nothing sophisticated, just a stew or boiled salt pork) before bringing it back to his messmates in a wooden bowl or bucket. Due to the difficulties of storing and preserving food aboard ship (canned meat, for example, was not available until 1816) the basic diet was very limited and consisted generally of salt pork and beef, together with dried peas, biscuits, oatmeal, sugar, butter and cheese, although the last two often went rancid if not properly stowed. It was not until the latter half of the 18th century that the value of fresh vegetables was fully appreciated although the beneficial effects of fruit juices were understood much earlier. Nelson was one of the earliest commanders to make proper arrangements for his ships to obtain fresh food and vegetables on a regular basis whenever possible and in particular his success in keeping his Mediterranean fleet extremely healthy while continually at sea for almost two years between 1803 and Trafalgar in 1805 ranks as one of his greatest, if unsung, achievements.

Opposite:
The towering stern of HMS *Victory* shows the layers of cabins where most of the officers were accommodated. The lowest level, in line with the middle gundeck, contained the wardroom and officers' cabins. Above that was the Admiral's accommodation including the great cabin which spanned the whole width of the deck. At the upper level, immediately below the poop, was the Captain's quarters, situated here so that he could be called on deck at a moment's notice. *ASM*

Above:
Part of Nelson's great cabin aboard the *Victory*. *ASM*

The warrant officers generally had their own small cabins, normally situated close to their particular activities. For example the Boatswain, Carpenter and Gunner would normally be forward where they had access to their stores while the Sailing Master might be in the so-called 'coach' houses under the poop deck, near the Captain's quarters. This arrangement is reflected today on ships such as the aircraft carrier *Invincible* where, for example, the Navigating Officer has a cabin immediately adjoining the Captain's sea cabin abaft the bridge.

The ship's commissioned officers, including those Marine officers on board, would all be housed in cabins in the after part of the ship, mostly at middle gundeck level with the exception of the midshipmen who were berthed in the gunroom at the after end of the lower gundeck. Also allocated cabins in this part of the ship would be the ship's surgeon, the chaplain and captain's secretary. The captain himself normally had a suite of cabins with accommodation for his servant or steward situated immediately below the poopdeck so that he could be instantly on deck if required, while in a three-decked First or Second Rate an admiral and his retinue would be accommodated in spacious cabins at the after end of the upper gundeck.

All these features, and much more, will be observed on a visit to HMS *Victory* as she lies in permanent drydock at Portsmouth in a remarkable state of preservation. In fact she is well over 200 years old having been laid down at Chatham on 23 July 1759, although she was not launched until May 1765 and subsequently lay uncompleted at anchor until 1778 when she was required for service in the War of American Independence. She had a reputation as a fast and comfortable sailer and was much in demand as a flagship, being used by several admirals before Nelson took her over in 1803 when she had just completed a major refit which had cost £70,000 — as much as it cost to build her in first place. After Trafalgar she underwent another major refit to repair the battle damage and recommissioned in 1808, serving almost continually until November 1812 when she returned to Portsmouth for the last time. Another major refit followed during which her bow was remodelled to provide more protection, her waist decked over and some iron knees used to strengthen the hull. However, by the time this work was completed the Napoleonic Wars were at an end and she was laid up in reserve, eventually becoming the static flagship of the C-in-C Portsmouth in 1824. Over the years she became a familiar sight in Portsmouth harbour and started to become something of a shrine to Nelson's memory but in 1903 she was seriously damaged when the battleship HMS *Neptune* accidentally rammed her, causing substantial damage. Although patched up, the ships timbers were deteriorating fast and after the end of World War 1 it was obvious that something had to be done before she rotted away altogether. Fortunately, enough funds were raised to enable her to be permanently berthed in the drydock at Portsmouth and for extensive renovation work to be carried out which was done between 1924 and 1928. The ship has been open to the public ever since and is still officially the flagship of the C-in-C Portsmouth who uses the ship for formal and ceremonial occasions.

Of Nelson's other ships virtually nothing remains, but a visit to the Bucklers Hard Maritime Museum near Beaulieu will reveal much about the first ship-of-the-line which he commanded, HMS *Agamemnon*. This 64-gun ship was actually built at Bucklers Hard and the site of the slipway where she was constructed and launched can still be seen. Inside the museum are various prints and documents relating to the ship and its history, and pride of place is given to a magnificent model of the *Agamemnon*. Also on view is a fascinating scale model diorama showing how the yard would have appeared a few days before the launch of the *Agamemnon* and much can be learned from this about how a ship-of-the-line was constructed using only basic handtools and varying

Above opposite:
Captain Hardy's cabin was just as sumptuous as Nelson's. Senior officers aboard a First Rate flagship lived in great style. *ASM*

Opposite:
The ordinary seaman lived, ate and slept around the guns. This shows a typical table and benches laid with wooden bowls and casks used for the storage of food and drink (water and grog!). In action all this would be cleared away to make room to man the guns. *ASM*

THE "VICTORY" IN PORTSMOUTH HARBOUR.

LORD NELSON

Above opposite:
Preserving HMS *Victory* is a full-time and never-ending job. Here, skilled shipwrights work on a new timber using tools unchanged from the 18th century. In fact only 15% of the ship's timbers are original, the rest having been replaced during various repairs and restorations. *ASM*

Opposite:
Contemporary postcard showing the *Victory* afloat in Portsmouth harbour at the beginning of this century. *Author's collection*

Top:
A model of HMS *Agamemnon*, Nelson's first ship-of-the-line, on display at Bucklers Hard where she was built. *ASM, by permission of the Curator, Bucklers Hard*

Above:
A fascinating tile mosaic to be found on the wall of 'The Nelson Arms' at Merton, Surrey. It shows HMS *Victory* as she was rebuilt after the Battle of Trafalgar. Bulwarks have been built up around the forecastle, and the waist between the forecastle and poop has been decked over. It is interesting to compare this with the ship as she stands today, having been rebuilt to her appearance at Trafalgar. *ASM*

baulks of timber. There were no machine tools in those days and virtually everything depended on hand or horse power. The *Agamemnon* itself had a long career following her launch in 1781 and Nelson commanded her from January 1793 until June 1796 during which time she took part in several engagements including the capture of the *Ça Ira* in 1795. At the end of her period in the Mediterranean she returned, without Nelson, to England for a refit but she was later present at the Battle of Copenhagen in 1801 and also at Trafalgar in 1805. After years of arduous service she was lost after running aground on a shoal in mouth of the River Plate off Montevideo in 1809. However, in recent years the site of the wreck has been located and examined by divers and as a result of this activity the museum at Bucklers Hard has on display a section of copper plate from the ship's bottom — a small but tangible fragment of one of Nelson's favourite ships.

After the Battle of the Nile in 1798, Nelson's own flagship, the *Vanguard*, was sorely in need of a refit and in June 1799 he transferred his flag to a brand new 80-gun two-decker, the *Foudroyant*. Launched in August 1798, it had originally been intended that she would be Nelson's flagship when he sailed for the Mediterranean earlier that year but delays in her completion meant that she was not ready until the following year from when she acted as his flagship until he left for home in the summer of 1800. Surprisingly, this ship had a long and active career and only an unfortunate accident prevented the ship from possibly still being afloat today. Her active service lasted until 1861 although for a while she was hulked at Plymouth and used as a gunnery training ship. In 1890 she was sold to a German company for breaking up but, before this could happen, she was bought from them by Mr G. W. Cobb of Chepstow who wanted to restore the ship to its former glory so that it could tour various coastal resorts and, at the same time, act as a sail training ship for youngsters. This far-sighted ideal was put into practice and the *Foudroyant* was extensively refitted between 1892 and 1897 when she set off on a fund-raising tour of the British coast. Surprisingly, considering that her naval crew would have been around 650 men, she was manned only by a crew of six together with a group of young boys under training. On 16 June she was driven ashore by a gale on to Blackpool sands and, although the crew were eventually rescued, the ship was deemed to be a total loss and was broken up on the spot. However, some relics of the ship can be seen today. For example, at Caldicot Castle near Chepstow can be seen the original figurehead together with one of the ship's cannons. In order to raise money, timber and copper from the wreck were used to make up all sorts of articles ranging from furniture to ashtrays, ping pong rackets and collar studs, which were widely sold at the time and may often be found today, particularly in the north-west around the Blackpool area. The Nelson museum at Monmouth has a magnificent carved bookcase made from the ship's timbers together with a small display relating to the ship, including some photographs of the wreck at Blackpool.

Another relic of the *Foudroyant* is one of the ship's cannons which stands alone on the grass ramparts above the Spur Redoubt at Portsmouth, overlooking the spot where Nelson embarked before Trafalgar. When the original *Foudroyant* was lost, Mr Cobb was not deterred from his grand scheme and purchased another ship, the *Trincomalee*, launched at Bombay Dockyard in 1817 and one of a class of 39 sailing frigates. Renamed *Foudroyant* in memory of the earlier ship, she had a much more successful second career and as recently as 1987 was still being used as a static training ship moored in Portsmouth harbour. By that time, there was a strong movement to preserve vital examples of Britain's maritime heritage and she was taken to Hartlepool where she is currently being completely rebuilt and restored to her original condition for eventual public display. However, back in 1972 while still moored at Portsmouth, it was discovered that much of the ship's ballast consisted of 40 cannons from the original *Foudroyant* and some of

Opposite:
This diorama model shows how the yard near Beaulieu would have appeared while the *Agamemnon* was under construction. In the background are the rows of workers' cottages which still stand today.
ASM, by permission of the Curator, Bucklers Hard

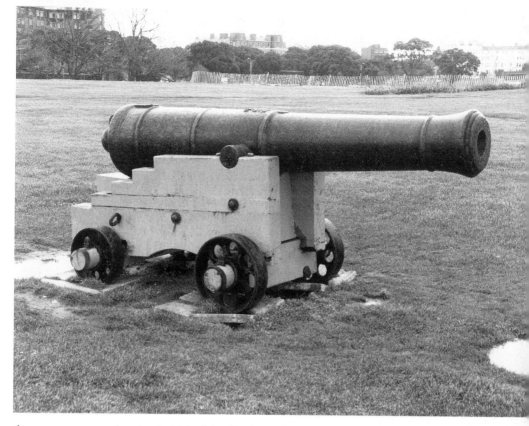

these were removed and refurbished for display. It is from this source that the lone example now standing at Portsmouth (and the one at Caldicot Castle) was obtained.

In Nelson's times the Royal Navy ranged far and wide across the oceans of the world and required a vast fleet in order to carry out its duties so that in 1801, for example, the strength of the Navy stood at over 850 ships and craft of all types. Although this figure included many minor vessels such as brigs, cutters, storeships and hulks, it also included 180 ships-of-the-line mounting 60 guns or more and 218 frigates and other ships carrying between 24 and 56 guns. It is a little realised fact that the organisation required to build and maintain this great fleet was the largest industrial concern in the country by a long way, employing over 15,000 men by the end of the Napoleonic wars. Almost all the larger ships-of-the-line were built at the various Royal Dockyards, and although a few were laid down at Plymouth and Portsmouth dockyards, the largest proportion came from the dockyards on the Thames and Medway. Smaller vessels, such as Fourth and Fifth Rates, as well as frigates and other craft, were often built by private contractors of which the Adams yard at Bucklers Hard where the *Agamemnon* was built is a typical example. Another private yard still in existence is Parson's yard at Burseldon in the upper reaches of the River Hamble, now named the Elephant yard after HMS *Elephant* which was Nelson's flagship at Copenhagen and was launched here in 1786. Today the small yard is exclusively concerned with the building and repair of small pleasure craft, but a discreet signpost at the entrance gives a clue to its historic past.

Of the three main Royal Dockyards, the most interesting in the context of this book is Chatham which finally closed as a Naval

Above opposite:
A view of Bucklers Hard today. The indentation in the foreshore is the site of the slipway where the *Agamemnon* was built. *ASM*

Opposite:
The drydock at Chatham where HMS *Victory* was built. *ASM*

Above:
This cannon, to be found on the ramparts of the old defences at Southsea, came from the *Foudroyant*, one of Nelson's flagships in the Mediterranean. Another can be found at Caldicot Castle, along with the ship's original figurehead. *ASM*

121

base in the 1980s. However, the part of the Dockyard used by the modern navy in the 20th century consisted mostly of an extension built since 1860 and the original dockyard area was subsequently left unchanged although the buildings were still in use. Consequently this area still stands today and was taken over by the Chatham Historic Dockyard Trust in 1984 for development as a living museum to enable visitors to get an insight into the organisation and running of a working dockyard in Nelson's time. Many of the buildings would have been familiar to him although there are also additions from later in the 19th century. Perhaps the most tangible connection is the No.2 drydock, originally constructed in 1623, where HMS *Victory* was laid down and built between 1759 and 1765 while the original sail loft where her sails were cut and made up still stands at the top of the rise overlooking the dock. Other buildings dating from Nelson's time include the Dockyard Commissioner's house, various workshops, the ornate and imposing main gate, and a magnificent terrace of officers' quarters.

Above:
The Dockyard Commissioner's house at Chatham was built in 1704 and is the oldest building in the present dockyard. It would have been a sight familiar to Nelson who passed through the dockyard on his way to join his first ship at the age of 12. *ASM*

Opposite:
Among the many buildings preserved at Chatham is this sail loft, built in 1734, where the sails for HMS *Victory* were made. Even today the loft is used by a company making sails for leisure craft. *ASM*

Also of significance are the imposing white sheds which formed the mast houses and moulding lofts, erected between 1753 and 1756. The moulding loft was where the lines of a ship were chalked out at full size so that templates could be cut and vital measurements taken during construction. It was here that the *Victory*'s lines were drawn out but the building now houses the excellent Wooden Walls exhibition and display which uses the latest museum audio visual technology to tell the story of the ordering, building, launching and commissioning of HMS *Valiant*, a typical 74 built at Chatham in 1758/59. This really is a worthwhile presentation which brings to life the comments and impressions of people who actually worked on the construction of the ship and were involved in the manning and sailing of her. The organisation required to build such a ship was remarkably sophisticated and

ELLIOTT PRODUCTS
SAILMAKERS
MEDWAY   408160

THE GUILD OF MASTER CRAFTSMEN

SAIL & COLOUR LOFT. Built 1734.
The Sails, Canvas Gear and Flags of
THE "VICTORY"
were Made in this Building

COLLEGE ROAD

well-established, and the Wooden Walls experience goes into great detail as well as providing information on the uses of the various buildings still standing in the dockyard.

Anyone who has visited both HMS *Victory* and the Chatham Historic dockyard will have seen much to illustrate the practical side of life in the Royal Navy in the days of Nelson and the way in which its ships were built, manned and fought. The artefacts and buildings on display have a real and tangible connection with Nelson as he would have been familiar with them all, but now that he is long since dead and gone, and his great fleets have almost completely disappeared, there is still much to see and find which was created to ensure that the memory of his glorious deeds is never lost.

Above:
Over a quarter of a mile long, the ropery at Chatham is still used for the manufacture of traditional ropes. A ship such as the *Victory* required around 20 miles of cordage for its rigging. *ASM*

Engraved by W.Deeble, from a Drawing by J.S.Cotman, for the Excursions through Norfolk.

N.W. View of
NELSON'S MONUMENT,
On the Denes Yarmouth,
NORFOLK.

Pub.d April 1. 1819 by Longman & C.o Paternoster Row.

5: THE IMMORTAL MEMORY

Nelson's dramatic death aboard the *Victory* at the very moment of his greatest triumph was the final act of a life and career which had already caught the public imagination to an unprecedented degree. Consequently there can be no surprise in discovering the variety and extent of the ways in which the memory of the man and his achievements have been perpetuated to this very day. The most obvious and public manifestation is in the various monuments and memorials erected in his honour, as well as others dedicated to the many officers and seamen who lost their lives fighting for their country under his command. Of these, Nelson's Column set in Trafalgar Square is the most prominent and significant but there are many more throughout the United Kingdom, some in places which would seem to have no obvious connection with the man and his battles.

For individuals, the memory of Nelson and his battles was often given tangible form in the shape of commemorative medals, all of which are avidly sought by collectors today. It was not until the mid-19th century that the British Army and Navy adopted a recognised system of medals and awards for bravery and conspicuous service. In 1846 the Naval General Service Medal was introduced and was awarded retrospectively to the survivors of Nelson's battles at Trafalgar and Copenhagen. In each case the blue and white ribbon on which the medal was hung also carried a bronze clasp with the name of the battle engraved on it. Prior to the introduction of official medals it had been the practice for private individuals to pay for the striking and distribution of commemorative medals to participants in various actions.

The most famous in Nelson's case were the Trafalgar medals struck by Alexander Davison, Nelson's agent and friend, and which were presented to all officers and seamen present at the battle. However, there were numerous other examples, several of which are described later in this chapter.

Even in his own lifetime, Nelson was a popular hero and almost all contemporary producers of glass, stoneware and porcelain brought out commemorative pieces in the form of plates, cups, mugs, glasses and figures to mark his various successes. Today's souvenir industry could teach little to the entrepreneurs of the time who showered the nation with memorabilia of varying quality and style. The death of Nelson in 1805 and the enormous interest in his state funeral was the cue for the production of further items, and various events since then have occasioned the commissioning of even more memorabilia — notably the official unveiling of Nelson's Column in

1846 and the centenary celebrations commemorating the Battle of Trafalgar in 1905. Today some of these items are much sought after by collectors and can command high prices.

Nelson also lives on through the many books which have been published about his life, together with the many analyses of his great battles. The first biographies appeared within a few months of Nelson's death and one, by Thomas Tegg, is reported to have sold over 50,000 copies at a price of 6d each. The first official biography was published in 1809 and was jointly written by James Clarke and John McArthur, the latter having served with Nelson as a purser. In 1813 Robert Southey, later to become poet laureate, wrote his acclaimed *The Life of Horatio Lord Nelson* and since that time there have been numerous other attempts at biographies although some later versions have benefited from access to various papers and documents which have gradually come to light. Today the most respected biography is that written by Carola Oman, simply titled *Nelson*, and first published in 1947. Among current authors, Tom Pocock's *Life of Nelson* is well thought of and benefits from the fruits of modern research.

Despite the fact that Nelson died before the age of photography, it is still possible to gain a very good impression of his actual appearance due the work of contemporary artists who produced a variety of fascinating portraits. Many of these are readily accessible today in institutions such as the National Portrait Gallery, the Royal Naval Museum at Portsmouth and the National Maritime Museum in Greenwich. The earliest authenticated portrait of Nelson was started when he was a young lieutenant, aged around 18 years, although not completed until a few years later when he returned from the West Indies as a Post Captain. This was painted by John

Previous page:
A contemporary print showing the Nelson Memorial at Great Yarmouth shortly after completion. *Author's Collection*

Above opposite:
Nelson's Column standing in Trafalgar Square, the best known of all Nelson monuments. *ASM*

Opposite:
Around the base of the column are four relief panels depicting scenes from Nelson's battles. This one shows him accepting the swords of the defeated Spanish commanders at the Battle of St Vincent. *ASM*

Above:
The panel commemorating Nelson's victory at Copenhagen. *ASM*

Left:
The mortally wounded Nelson is carried from the deck of the *Victory* at Trafalgar. This poignant scene is portrayed on one of the panels at the base of Nelson's Column. *ASM*

Rigaud but he was followed by a number of artists of varying talent and techniques of which Lemuel Abbott is perhaps the most popular. Of course, ordinary people of the time would not have had access to these paintings which were private commissions and to satisfy demand engravers would produce prints for sale to the public. Some of these faithfully reproduced the various paintings and many were hand-coloured. Today such prints can command high prices, but bargains can be had by the collector who is prepared to spend time and effort searching through antique and print shops around the country. Naturally, the original paintings are priceless and all are in public or private collections.

The names of Nelson and his contemporaries and his achievements have been kept alive through the years within the Royal Navy by the naming of various ships and shore establishments. Currently HMS *Nelson* is the title of the Naval Base at Portsmouth while the fleet also lists HMS *Trafalgar*, a nuclear-powered hunter killer submarine, among its present strength. Of course, it is much more than just the name which is venerated in the Navy which also continues to lay great stress on the combination of intelligence, flair, courage, foresight and emphasis on teamwork which was the key to Nelson's success in battle. In 1941, during World War 2, the Royal Navy was under intense pressure in the Mediterranean during the evacuation of troops from Greece and Crete. Many senior officers held the opinion that the Navy could not continue to sustain the serious losses of ships and men and suggested that the evacuations should be abandoned. Admiral Cunningham, commanding the Mediterranean Fleet, must have had Nelson very much in mind when he said, ' It takes three years to build a new ship, but three hundred years to build a tradition'. The Navy continued the evacuation until every soldier who could reach the coast had been taken off.

In a lighter vein, the name of Nelson, his associates, his ships and battles are commemorated throughout the land in the form of pubs, inns, hotels and other establishments bearing these titles. This form of memorial alone could form the basis of a lifetime hobby if one had the time to track them all down. A few examples given later in this chapter must suffice as an introduction to this fascinating aspect of tracking down the Nelson connection.

Memorials

Every tourist and visitor to London must be familiar with the icon that is Nelson's Column, set in the open space of Trafalgar Square in the centre of the capital. Overlooking all is the statue of Nelson, facing south along Whitehall and peering forever into the distance towards the south coast and the English Channel where he embarked on so many of his great endeavours. The decision to formally commemorate Nelson was followed by a competition to design the most fitting memorial and this inspired several ideas, including one suggestion that HMS *Victory*, then still afloat, should be brought to London and transported to the site of the square! However, the design submitted by William Railton, a leading architect of the time, was finally chosen although the statue was the subject of a

separate commission, awarded to the sculptor
E. H. Bailey RA. The initial contract was awarded to
Messrs Grissel and Peto in 1838 and in 1840 the
foundation stone, a 14 ton block of Dartmoor granite,
was laid by one Charles Davison Scott, the son of John
Scott who was secretary to Nelson at Trafalgar and who
was also killed in the battle. Buried under the stone is a
sealed bottle containing Victorian coins and a parchment
which records the work of the Committee and Trustees
appointed to oversee the design and building of the
monument. The actual column itself is made up of
granite blocks each weighing 9 tons and is 120ft high,
finished in the fluted Corinthian style. On top of this is a
metal capital or pedestal on which the statue is mounted.
The figure of Nelson was carved from three blocks of
Craigleth stone which together originally weighed 30
tons, although the final statue actually weighs 16 tons
and stands 17ft 4in high. It was hoisted into place on 3
and 4 November 1843. The massive figure is 5ft 3in
across at the shoulders while the sword at his side is 7ft
long and his hat is 4ft high!

In 1852 four bronze bas-relief panels were mounted
on the sides of the base pedestal, each depicting the
scene at one of Nelson's four famous battles (Trafalgar,
Copenhagen, the Nile and St Vincent). Although each is
depicted in a similar heroic style, they are actually the work of different artists. The four
lions flanking the base of the column were not added until 1868 and were the work of Sir
Edwin Landseer. Although Trafalgar Square today is an open area surrounded by
imposing public buildings, at the time of its construction the area was one of London's
worst slums and the scheme for the memorial to Nelson and Trafalgar was intended to
provide a more fitting vista in the centre of the Nation's capital — an aim which was
certainly achieved. The final cost was over £50,000 of which £30,000 came from the
government and the rest from public and private subscriptions.

Despite its age, the monument is in good condition. It is cleaned and refurbished at
periods of around 20 years. This was last done in 1987, having previously been renovated
in 1967, 1946, 1919, and 1905. The main problems are preventing water getting into the
stonework and eroding it, and clearing off the accumulation of bird
droppings, which can build up to layers over 10in thick in places! As

Opposite:
The figure of Britannia at
the top of the Yarmouth
memorial. *ASM*

Above:
The Nelson Memorial at
Great Yarmouth was
completed in 1819. *ASM*

Left:
When built, the memorial
at Yarmouth stood on an
open spit of land between
the sea and the River
Yare. Today it is
surrounded by the
anonymous buildings of
an industrial estate,
although a pub called
'The Nelson' stands
nearby. *ASM*

part of the Trafalgar centenary celebrations in 1905, the column was covered with extensive decorations which included a rope of laurel circling around it in a spiral, with similar ropes running from the top of the column, around the lions and back up again. A flag flew at the top, just below the statue, and naval flags spelt out the famous signal, 'England expects ...'.

Outside London there are several memorials to Nelson and one of the most significant is at Great Yarmouth on the Norfolk coast where Nelson landed on his return from Naples following his overland journey across Europe. It was also from here that he set off for the Baltic and subsequent fame at the Battle of Copenhagen and so it was entirely appropriate as a site for memorial, especially as Nelson was born in Norfolk. In fact the first suggestion for a memorial was made immediately following Trafalgar and by March 1806 the sum of £800 had been collected to fund a scheme for a monument in Norwich, the county capital. However, this plan was not executed and in 1814 a new subscription was opened and a site at South Denes, Great Yarmouth, was selected. The following year, a design for a column by William Wilkins was approved and the foundation stone laid at a grand ceremony by Col Wodehouse, chairman of the monument committee, in August 1817. There was a procession by the mayor and civic dignitaries from the town hall, escorted by the band of the East Norfolk Militia, and a copper plaque together with various gold and silver coins were buried beneath the foundations.

The monument was completed in 1819 and the tall column was also intended to act as a seamark to assist ships in their navigation along the Norfolk coast. Built of white Mansfield stone, it stands 144ft high and is in the form of a fluted Doric column mounted on a square pedestal which, in turn, stands on a terraced base. At the top of the column is a podium upon which stand a number of figures supporting a cupola on which is mounted the figure of Britannia facing to the west. On the four sides of the capital at the top of the column are inscribed the names of some of Nelson's ships (*Vanguard, Captain, Elephant, Victory*) and at the top of the pedestal are the names of his famous victories (Aboukir, St Vincent, Copenhagen, Trafalgar). Other inscriptions record the names of the architect, committee members, contractor and superintendent of the works, while on the west side is an elaborate inscription in Latin by William Frere praising Nelson, cataloguing his battles and recording his connections with Norfolk.

Inside the column is a circular staircase (217 steps) which leads to a viewing gallery at the top of the column. Unfortunately this feature led on June 1819 to the death of the Town Surveyor, Thomas Sutton, who collapsed after climbing the staircase for a tour of inspection. In 1863 an acrobat called Marsh climbed out on to the figure of Britannia but lost his footing and fell to his death when he attempted to come down. When the

Right:
The monument to Nelson on Portsdown hill was built with money raised from those who fought at Trafalgar. *ASM*

Above opposite:
The inscription on the Portsdown memorial. *ASM*

monument was erected, a small cottage was built nearby to house a caretaker and the first holder of this post was one James Sharman who had served as a seaman aboard the *Victory* at the Battle of Trafalgar. Indeed he claimed to have assisted in carrying Nelson down to the cockpit where he subsequently died. Sharman remained in this post until he died in 1867 but he lives on in the pages of the famous novel by Charles Dickens, *David Copperfield*. It is reputed that Dickens met Sharman while on a visit to Yarmouth and subsequently based the character of Ham Peggoty and the shipwreck described in the book on Sharman and his experiences in 1829 when he helped to rescue a crew member from the brig *Hammond*, wrecked on Yarmouth beach.

Visitors to Yarmouth today may be able to enter the column and climb to the top where a panoramic view of the coast and inland over Norfolk can be gained. The monument is open during July and August, daily (except Saturdays) between 2pm and 6pm. There is a small admittance charge and for organised party visits, access can be arranged at other times of the year. On 21 October, Trafalgar Day, each year the monument is dressed overall with signal flags spelling Nelson's well-known Trafalgar signal.

Not perhaps on the scale of the foregoing magnificent monuments are a number of nevertheless significant memorials scattered around the country. On the ridge of Portsdown Hill, overlooking Portsmouth Harbour, the Solent and Isle of Wight is a tall column bearing a relief bust of Nelson at its top. The foundation stone of this monument was laid in 1807 and it is of particular significance as the project was partly financed by the officers, seamen and marines who actually fought at Trafalgar and who each gave up two days' pay as a contribution. The inscription on the plinth forming the base reads:

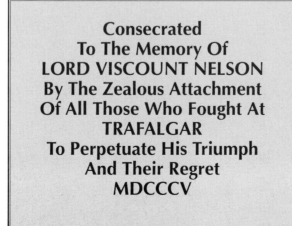

**Consecrated
To The Memory Of
LORD VISCOUNT NELSON
By The Zealous Attachment
Of All Those Who Fought At
TRAFALGAR
To Perpetuate His Triumph
And Their Regret
MDCCCV**

Another monument, less well-known but having a personal connection with Nelson, is that erected by his friend and agent Alexander Davison at Swarland in Northumberland. This is a simple obelisk and was erected in 1807 alongside the Great North Road which led from Newcastle to Edinburgh although today, a slight rerouteing of the main A1 trunk road means that the monument stands in peaceful solitude. It was originally almost 40ft high and stands on a 9ft square base, but it was struck by lightning many years ago and several feet were lost off the top. Near the lower part of the tapering obelisk are the inscriptions 'England expects that every man will do his duty' and 'Victory, 21st October, 1805'. However the largest plaque, on the base, contains a much more personal message as shown on this page

> **Not to commemorate the public virtues and heroic achievements of NELSON which is the duty of England: But to the memory of Private Friendship this erection is dedicated by ALEXANDER DAVISON. Swarland Hall.**

In many ways, because of its private and intimate nature, this simple memorial is more moving than many of the grand public monuments to be seen. Davison also commissioned a much more unusual memorial, and one which is only visible in its true form from the air. This consists of a plantation of trees on the estate of Swarland Hall, itself long since demolished, in the shape of the layout of Aboukir Bay, the site of Nelson's great victory over the French fleet in 1798. Looking down on the trees, the sweep of the bay can be clearly seen, while a small copse marks the Aboukir Island at the head of the bay. Stretching up from the lower corner are a line of trees, each tree representing the various ships in the battle, many of these having been replanted in recent years. This form of memorial is not entirely unique as there is a slightly better known planting on the Marquis of Queensberry's estate in Wiltshire in which the trees represent ships at the Battle of Trafalgar. Coming back to Swarland, it is interesting to note that there is a street in the village named after Emma Hamilton and a memorial to Davison can be found on Lanton Hill in the nearby Cheviot Hills.

Continuing northwards along the A1, there are two significant memorials to Nelson to be found in Scotland and the best known of these is on Calton Hill in Edinburgh where it shares a site overlooking the eastern end of Princes Street with another monument commemorating the Duke of Wellington and the Battle of Waterloo. Nelson's monument is a tower standing 106ft high and built in the form of an upturned telescope. As Calton Hill itself is 456ft above sea level, the view from the top of the tower is most impressive and well worth climbing the 170 steps of the spiral staircase in order to reach the lookout platform. A further flight of steps leads to a smaller platform at the very peak of the tower where a mechanical time signal was installed in 1852. This takes the form of a mechanism which raises a large time ball to the top of a short mast which then drops at 12 o'clock noon (GMT) every day. During the summer, a one o'clock (BST) time gun is fired from the ramparts of Edinburgh Castle, coinciding with the fall of the ball. The Calton tower was designed by the architect Robert Burn and work began in 1807 when a foundation stone was laid by the Lord Provost of Edinburgh on the second anniversary of Trafalgar. However, as the pace of work depended on the flow of public subscriptions which financed the project, it was not completed until 1815.

A less well-known memorial, perhaps because of its remote location, is that at Forres, on the Morayshire coast some 25 miles east of Inverness. Known as the Nelson Tower, this takes the form of a 70ft high octagonal tower erected as early as 1806 and was built using funds raised locally by a specially formed 'Trafalgar Club'.

Opposite left:
The Portsdown Memorial features a bust of Nelson at the top, but you will need binoculars or a telescope to see it in detail! *ASM*

Opposite right:
Near the memorial at Portsdown stands Fort Nelson, part of the chain of fortifications built to protect Portsmouth and its dockyards in the 1860s. *ASM*

Above:
Davison's personal memorial to Nelson stands just off the A1 in Northumberland. *ASM*

Left:
A most unusual memorial to Nelson is this group of trees planted by his friend Alexander Davison at Swarland in Northumberland. The trees enclosing the open space represent the Egyptian coast and the Bay of Aboukir, while the copse in the centre is Aboukir Island. The straight row of trees in the foreground represents the disposition of the ships at the Battle of the Nile. *ASM*

Standing on top of Cluny Hill, the tower has a diameter of 24ft and there are three floors plus a viewing gallery at the top from which a panoramic view across the Moray Firth to the north and the Grampian mountains to the south can be obtained. With the demise of the Trafalgar Club, the tower passed into the hands of the local authority in 1851 and like many monuments it was allowed to fall into disrepair for many years, although recently it has been restored to something of its former glory and and is now open to public viewing.

The only large monument to Nelson in Wales is sited on the banks of the Menai Strait near its north-east end. It was unveiled on 13 September 1873 and was commissioned by Admiral Clarence Lord Paget, KCB who at one time had risen to be C-in-C of the Mediterranean Fleet, a post formerly held by Nelson himself. The memorial takes the form of a square plinth surmounted by a pedestal which carries a statue of Nelson, the whole standing 41ft above the rock on which it is constructed. A door on the north side opens on to a ladder by which access can be gained to the parapet surrounding the central pedestal. Among the brief inscriptions on the monument, one on the east side carries the words 'Fell at Trafalgar 1805' while this is repeated in Welsh on the west side ('A Lladdwyd yn Trafalgar 1805'). At the time of its construction the exact site was determined by a suggestion from the Admiralty that the prominent memorial would form an excellent seamark for vessels navigating the Menai Strait and to this day it is shown on Admiralty charts and is used by yachtsmen and sailors for that purpose. Apart from the Menai memorial, there is also the Naval Temple at Monmouth, but this has been described earlier in the book and, in any case, it is not solely dedicated to Nelson as it commemorates no less than 16 British admirals and their battles.

Finally, it is not only in the United Kingdom that memorials to Nelson exist. In particular there is a fine statue of Nelson mounted on a 50ft column in Montreal, Canada. Being in a predominantly French-speaking part of the country, it is rather surprising to find the scourge of the French fleet commemorated in this way and indeed there was an attempt in recent times to have the statue removed. However, it was refurbished in 1980 and stands in the Place Jacques Cartier, at the heart of the old city, facing the town hall. In fact this monument was one of the earliest of its kind to be erected, the cornerstone being laid in 1809, only four years after Trafalgar, and it was built to a design prepared by a London architect named Mitchell. Originally there were engraved tablets commemorating the battles of Trafalgar, Copenhagen and the Nile but these were replaced by granite panels when the monument was refurbished in 1900. The original tablets are now preserved at the Château Ramezay.

The list of monuments described in the foregoing should not be taken as exhaustive although it does describe those which are the most well known, particularly significant or well preserved. There are more to be found, many in unexpected places, some of which will be simple stones while others will be quite ornate statues. Indeed at least one statue can be found in Taiwan, having been originally commissioned (along with a similar statue of the Duke of Wellington) by a Scottish businessman in 1836 for his new house being built in Edinburgh's upmarket Morningside district. In 1909 they were sold to the owner of a house at Coldstream, on the Scottish border, where they stood until 1987 and were subsequently sold at auction in 1992, the Nelson example going to the unnamed gentleman from Taiwan for the sum of £15,000 (students of Nelson will be pleased to learn that the Duke of Wellington fetched only £12,000!).

Medals

During Nelson's time there was not a recognised system of awarding medals such as pertains in the armed forces today. Commanders victorious in land or sea campaigns could expect honours in the form of peerages and knighthoods, although sometimes gold or silver medals were ordered to be struck and awarded to senior officers and captains. There was rarely any official medal for ordinary soldiers or seamen. One of the first official awards was the Navy Gold Medal instituted in 1795 and this was struck in two sizes (55mm and 32mm) for Flag Officers and Captains respectively. Nelson received two such medals for his part in the battles of St Vincent and the Nile and these will often be seen, suspended from ribbons around his neck, in paintings and sculptures of him. Unfortunately the originals were stolen in 1900 and have not been seen since.

However, junior officers and ordinary seamen were not totally forgotten as rich patrons or businessmen often took it upon themselves to pay for the striking and distribution of medals to commemorate various actions. The best known examples of this type of medal are those struck by Alexander Davison who made his fortune out of government contacts for military and naval stores. After the Battle of the Nile he commissioned a design which was produced in gold for Nelson and his captains, silver for lieutenants and warrant officers, gilt-copper for petty officers, and copper for seamen and marines. The total cost was around £2,000 although Davison could well afford this as he was appointed prize agent for the ships captured by Nelson at the battle. The obverse, or front, of the medal showed an allegorical figure representing Hope who is holding an olive branch in one hand and supporting a profile of Nelson with the other. Inscribed were the words 'Europe's Hope and Glory' and 'Rear-Admiral Lord Nelson of the Nile'. On the reverse is engraved a view of the British fleet approaching the French ships anchored in Aboukir Bay surrounded by the inscription 'Almighty God has blessed His Majesty's arms', while the words 'Victory of the Nile, August 1, 1798' appear below the scene. Specimens of these medals can be seen in several museums and are often engraved with the recipient's name and/or the name of the ship taking part in the battle.

There were a number of other medals struck to celebrate the victory at the Nile but most of these were of the commemorative type and intended for purchase by private individuals, although it is likely that some were bought by the participants or their families. Again these will often be found in various museums.

Opposite:
The Naval Temple at Monmouth commemorates the exploits of 16 British admirals, including Nelson, and was completed in 1802. *ASM*

After the Battle of the Nile Nelson became embroiled in the activities of the Court of King Ferdinand IV at Naples and following that monarch's restoration to the throne in 1799 a medal was struck at the suggestion of Matthew Boulton, proprietor of the Soho Mint in Birmingham. Records show that a total of 915 such medals were struck including 24 in silver and 12 in gilt, the rest being bronze or tin. Nelson received at least one of these medals although in a characteristically generous gesture he gave it the Commandant of the Danish Naval Academy which he had visited immediately after the Battle of Copenhagen. He subsequently obtained a replacement but it appears likely that this was stolen from Greenwich in 1900. However, other examples exist and can be seen at the National Maritime Museum which holds several in its extensive collections. Others are in the British Museum, the Ashmolean Museum and the National Museum of San Martino, Naples.

No official medals were ever issued to mark the victory over the Danish fleet at Copenhagen in 1801 although Nelson was rewarded with a Viscountcy and received orders and decorations from Germany and the Turkish Sultan Selim III. Despite this, Nelson was angered at the lack of recognition for the bravery of his men and tried hard to gain them some official recognition, However, the government did not want to be seen to be too exultant over the result of a battle which probably could have been avoided by better diplomacy in the first place. Nor did they want to upset the Danes and the Russians, or offend the Swedes who remained a powerful force in the Baltic. There were a small number of private medals produced and at one point Alexander Davison announced his intention to strike medals for the participants as he had with the Battle of the Nile but this plan was not implemented. It was for his actions at Copenhagen that Nelson was awarded the German Order of St Joachim.

Above:
A typical medal of the type struck to commemorate the victory at the Battle of the Nile. This particular example by an unknown artist was struck in copper/bronze although there are also a few to be found in silver. *National Maritime Museum*

The aftermath of Trafalgar was naturally greeted with a flood of commemorative medals, some official and others being for private circulation. A posthumous award of the Navy Gold Medal was made to Nelson but was lost to posterity when it was stolen, along with his other medals, from Greenwich in 1900. However, all the participating captains were awarded the small Gold Medal and many of these can be seen at museum displays today including those of Captain George Duff of HMS *Mars* and Captain R. Grindal, HMS *Prince*. For the seaman and other officers, the most commonly seen is that struck by Matthew Boulton which featured a profile of Nelson on the obverse with a general view of the battle taken from a sketch by Richard Cleveley on the reverse which also carried the words of Nelson's signal around the edge. These medals were variously struck in gold, silver, copper/bronze and copper gilt and a staggering total of over 14,000 were produced with the intention of giving one to every man who had taken part. As a consequence of this greater quantity, they are not uncommon and examples can be seen at all the relevant museums.

A much rarer medal is one, believed to have been commissioned by Davison for issue to the officers and men of the *Victory*, which is cast in white metal and features a broadside view of the *Victory* on one side and a bust of Nelson on the other. Inevitably the words of the famous signal appear on the reverse while the obverse bears an inscription of which part includes a fascinating biblical reference 'The Lord is a Man of War/ Exodus C.15.v.3.'! In addition to this there are at least half a dozen other Trafalgar medals to be seen and yet more produced to commemorate the Death of Nelson and his funeral. Other medals were produced to mark various occasions throughout the next century including some struck for presentation to the Royal Marine guard of honour at the official opening ceremony of Nelson's Column in 1844 and also to some 350 survivors of Nelson's various battles who were incumbent at the Naval Hospital, Greenwich at the time. These were struck in pewter and carried a bust of Nelson, together with the words of his signal on the obverse and a view of Trafalgar Square on the reverse. A description of all the medals produced with a Nelson connection would fill a book; indeed a book has been written on this very subject, and there is certainly not enough space here. However, readers will find most of those already described, together with many others, contained in the various museum collections.

The Name Lives On

The Royal Navy traditionally perpetuates the names of its heroes and their battles in the naming of its warships and, as might be expected, that of Nelson has been marked in this way. The first HMS *Nelson* was a magnificent 120-gun three-decker, well worthy of the name, laid down at Woolwich in 1809 but not launched until 1814, too late to be of effective use in the Napoleonic Wars which ended the following year. After a period of undistinguished service, she was converted to a screw line-of-battleship in 1860. This involved cutting her in half and lengthening the hull, removing the upper gundeck and installing engines and boilers. Many of the old sailing warships were so converted around this time, but such was the pace of technological development that they were obsolete before the work was completed and the *Nelson* was subsequently sold to the New South Wales government in Australia in 1867 where she served as a coast defence ship, training ship and floating gun battery before being paid off in 1891. She survived as a floating store until being finally broken up at Tasmania in 1928.

The next HMS *Nelson* was one of a pair of armoured frigates, 280ft long and displacing 7,360 tons, launched in 1876 and armed with four 10in and eight 9in muzzle-loading rifled guns as well as half a dozen 20-pounders. Coincidentally this ship saw several years' service in Australian waters before returning home for a refit in 1889. She

paid off in 1901 and became a static training hulk attached to the Stoker's Training Establishment at Portsmouth before being sold off to Dutch shipbreakers in 1910.

In the first decade of the 20th century, the Royal Navy was engaged in a massive arms race with the nascent German Navy and the result was a steady increase in the size and numbers of heavily armed and armoured battleships. In 1906 the two newest, and largest, in a line of development going back to the Majestic class of 1894, were launched bearing the names *Agamemnon* and *Lord Nelson*. Displacing 16,500 tons, the two ships made 18kt on coal-fired triple expansion steam engines and were armed with four 12in and 10 9.2in breech loading guns together with numerous 12-pounder quick firing weapons. Unfortunately these ships were obsolete even as they were being built as battleship design was altered at a stroke by the appearance of HMS *Dreadnought* in the same year, this 18,000ton ship being powered by the latest steam turbines giving 21kt and mounting the prodigious armament of 10 12in guns. All subsequent battleship construction concentrated on improved versions of the *Dreadnought* and the older pre-dreadnoughts (as they were termed) such as HMS *Nelson* found themselves employed in secondary duties when World War 1 broke out in 1914. Nevertheless, HMS *Nelson* distinguished herself in the Mediterranean, taking part in the abortive Dardanelles operation and supporting the bloody landings at Gallipoli. After the war she was laid up and sold for scrapping in 1921.

In the years between the wars, naval construction by the world's great powers was regulated by various treaties and as a result of the 1921 Washington Naval Treaty, Britain was permitted to build two new battleships armed with the new 16in guns and displacing not

Above:
The 35,000 ton battleship *Nelson*, launched in 1925, was the fourth major ship to bear the name. Armed with nine 16in guns, she and her sister ship (*Rodney*) carried the heaviest armament of any British battleships.
Author's collection

Above opposite:
The battle honours of HMS *Nelson* are proudly displayed at the entrance to the base. Notice that the name has been borne by a number of small craft in addition to the powerful battleships.
ASM

Opposite:
The name 'Nelson' is today borne by a shore establishment at Portsmouth Naval Base.
ASM

more than 35,000 tons. The two ships, named *Nelson* and *Rodney*, were launched in 1925 and at the outbreak of World War 2 were the most powerful battleships in the Royal Navy. However, with a speed of only 22kt, they were much slower than the new battleships then being completed by all the major naval powers, including Britain, and consequently they could play only a limited role in the forthcoming struggle. Nevertheless, HMS *Nelson* had an active war although she was heavily damaged by a magnetic mine in December 1939 which put her out of action for several months. Later she played a distinguished part in the Mediterranean where she escorted Malta convoys as part of Force H and supported the invasions of North Africa, Sicily and Salerno. Appropriately, the armistice with Italy was signed aboard her in Malta on 29 September 1943, the first of the Axis powers to be defeated. After returning to the UK to support the D-Day landings in Normandy, she was sent to the United States for a major refit, after which she served as flagship of the British Eastern Fleet based on Ceylon until the end of 1945. After the war, HMS *Nelson* served as a training ship before being paid off in 1948 and being scrapped the following year. As recounted in Chapter 2, her ensigns and a copy of the ship's crest were presented to All Saints' church at Nelson's birthplace in Norfolk.

In recent years there have been no ships to perpetuate the memory of Nelson, but the name is now borne by the naval accommodation and administration establishment at Portsmouth Naval Base. HMS *Nelson*, a stone frigate in naval parlance, is sited on the south side of the dockyard area, immediately adjacent to the area surrounding HMS *Victory*. At the main entrance the name is boldly emblazoned while just inside the gate stands a figurehead carved in the likeness of Nelson as he would have been at the time of the Battle of the Nile in 1798, wearing the uniform of a Rear-Admiral. This figurehead was actually made in 1938 for the training ship HMS *Conway* to replace one damaged in a collision. *Conway* herself was originally HMS *Nile*, a 90-gun two-decker launched in 1839 and named to commemorate Nelson's famous victory. She was converted to steam power in 1854 and was paid off in 1876 when she became a training hulk and was renamed *Conway* when lent to the Mercantile Marine Association of Liverpool. In 1953 she ran aground in the Menai Strait and the wreck was finally burnt in 1956. The *Conway* training establishment was moved ashore and retained the figurehead until 1974 when it closed. At the present day HMS *Nelson*, another relic of days gone by is the Battle Honours Board from the World War 2 battleship of the same name which is mounted on the wall of the guardhouse for all visitors to see. The honours associated with the name, all won by the same ship, are:

Malta Convoys	**1941-42**
North Africa	**1942-43**
Mediterranean	**1943**
Sicily	**1943**
Salerno	**1943**
Normandy	**1944**

The first HMS *Nile* has already been mentioned, but there was another. This was a turret battleship launched in 1888 (one of two) which carried four 13.5in guns in twin turrets fore and aft, and a battery of six 4.7in guns amidships. On a displacement of 12,589 tons she made 15kt and her appearance was distinguished by low freeboard and twin side-by-side funnels. She was typical of the first generation of battleships to mount their breech loading guns in turrets and to rely entirely on steam propulsion. Nevertheless she was obsolete long before the outbreak of World War 1 and was sold off for scrapping in 1912. The name *Nile* was allocated to a shore establishment at Alexandria in 1939 but has not been used since the end of World War 2.

Opposite:
This magnificent figurehead in the likeness of Nelson originally came from HMS *Nile*, launched in 1839. It subsequently became a training ship and the figurehead passed to various shore establishments before ending up at Portsmouth. *ASM*

Nelson's famous victory at Trafalgar was also marked and the name is actually in use today. It was first allocated in 1806 to a 110-gun three-decker ordered that year, although the ship was not laid down until 1813 and was then completed in 1820. Renamed *Camperdown* in 1825, she saw several years' service before being hulked in 1860 and later became a coal depot at Portsmouth. She was renamed yet again in 1882, becoming the *Pitt*, before being sold off and broken up in 1906. The second *Trafalgar* was a 120-gun three-decker First Rate launched in 1841 and, among other duties, she took part in the Crimean War during 1854. Like many of the largest and newest ships-of-the-line she was converted to stream propulsion in 1859 but was renamed *Boscawen* in 1873 and was finally sold off in 1906. A remnant of this ship can still be seen by visitors to HMS *Victory* as the original ship's figurehead, carved in the likeness of Lord Nelson, is on display adjacent to the ticket kiosk. One reason for the renaming of the second *Trafalgar* was to release the name for a new battleship, launched in 1887, a sister ship to the second HMS *Nile* already described. She had a similar career and was sold off for scrapping in 1911.

H.M.S. TRAFALGAR, 120 GUNS.

Printed & Published at G. J. Cox's Litho Estabm.t Royal Polytechnic, London.

The name *Trafalgar* was revived during World War 2 for a destroyer launched in 1944. This was one of the 'Battle' class destroyers, the best of their type produced by Britain during the war. However, most of them were completed too late to see any action, although they provided the backbone of the peacetime flotillas for over a decade after the end of the war. HMS *Trafalgar* was one of the first batch to be completed but did not reach the Far East until after VJ Day although she remained in eastern waters until 1947 when she returned home and paid off into reserve. The ship did recommission until 1958 when she became leader of the 7th Destroyer Squadron and deployed to Home and Mediterranean waters until finally paying off in 1963. After several more years in reserve, she was scrapped in 1970.

The newest *Trafalgar* is an entirely different type of ship, a nuclear-powered hunter killer submarine launched in 1981 and the first of a class of seven similar vessels. Displacing over 5,000 tons when submerged, the modern HMS *Trafalgar* is armed with long-range Spearfish and Tigerfish torpedoes, as well as sub-Harpoon, a submarine launched anti-ship missile with a range of around 90 miles. Its nuclear powerplant can drive it at over 30kt when submerged and, packed with the latest electronic devices, these submarines are today's capital ships — the true successors to Nelson's sailing ships-of-the-line of two centuries ago.

Over the years there have been a number of other names given to Royal Navy ships which also have a Nelson connection although there are few, if any, in the Royal Navy of today. A notable one is *St Vincent*, applied to a First Rate of 1815 and a battleship of 1908, before being used by a shore establishment from 1927. *Collingwood* is another name also given to a similar progression of ships and finally perpetuated by a shore establishment. Many of Nelson's captains have given their names to ships and several of the ships present at Trafalgar have had their names perpetuated. Several of the recently-retired 'Leander' class frigates carried names proudly borne at Trafalgar including *Euryalus*, *Naiad*, *Phoebe*, *Sirius*, and *Ajax*. In the present fleet is HMS *Swiftsure*, nameship of the five similar nuclear-powered hunter killer submarines which preceded the Trafalgar class, and this name was borne by 74 in Collingwood's column at Trafalgar.

Above opposite:
Another figurehead to feature Nelson; this one came from HMS *Trafalgar*, launched in 1841, and now stands alongside the *Victory*. *ASM*

Opposite:
The second HMS *Trafalgar*, a 120-gun First Rate which took part in the Crimean War before being converted to steam propulsion. *Author's Collection*

Above:
The present HMS *Trafalgar* is a nuclear-powered hunter killer submarine — one of today's capital ships and a far cry from the wooden sailing ships which Nelson knew so well. *RN*

A Drop of Nelson's Blood

The most common form of Nelson Memorial, and one which most people will come across at one time or another, results from the British tradition of naming their public houses and inns after famous people and events. Hidden away in every major town will be found at least one 'Lord Nelson', or 'Victory', or 'Trafalgar Inn' while in places with an obvious link, such as Norfolk or Portsmouth, it seems that every other pub has a Nelson connotation. There is some debate as to which is the oldest Nelson pub but it would

appear that one with a good claim is the 'Lord Nelson' at Fulstow in Lincolnshire. Documentary evidence exists to show that this inn was called the 'Lord Nelson' as far back as May 1804, over a year before Nelson's death at Trafalgar, and it was in continuous use until 1971 when it closed, although the actual building still exists as a private house. Another establishment which might be thought to have a good claim is the 'Lord Nelson' at Burnham Thorpe, Nelson's birthplace, but this was originally called 'The Plough' and did not adopt its present name until 1807. There is another 'Lord Nelson' at nearby Burnham Sutton but, although built in the 18th century, it was not renamed until 1810. One of the earliest pubs to adopt the name after Nelson's death was the 'Lord Nelson' inn at Nelson in Lancashire where a new pub of that name opened at a busy road junction in 1805. Indeed it is claimed that the present town took its name from this source.

There is an amusing tale told of the 'Wrestler's Inn' at Great Yarmouth where Nelson stayed when he reached England in 1800 after travelling overland from Italy, and again after the Battle of Copenhagen. Appraised of a plan to rename the inn 'The Nelson Arms' in his honour, he is said to have remarked, 'That would be absurd, seeing as I have only one arm!'. This inn still stands on the edge of the market square at Great Yarmouth but it is now called 'Hardy's', a name which modern market research no doubt has decided has a contemporary ring to it while still retaining a Nelson connection. In fact there is a 'Nelson Arms' at Merton in Surrey where he set up home with Emma Hamilton in 1802 and this is decorated with fine tile mosaics showing Nelson and the *Victory*.

There are several variations to be seen in pub titles relating to the Nelson name. Apart from the 'Nelson Arms', 'Lord Nelson', 'Admiral Nelson' and even just 'The Nelson' are quite common and several pubs bearing names such as 'The Admiral' or 'The Hero' normally relate to Nelson and often include his portrait on their signs. The latter name is particularly common in his home county of Norfolk, indeed there as a 'Hero' at Overy Staithe where Nelson would have had his first sight of the sea. Other Nelson pubs crop up in the most unlikely places which would seem to have no apparent connection with him at all. A typical example can be found at Thirsk in North Yorkshire where there is an excellent pub called 'The Lord Nelson' whose sign bears a very good portrait of him in full dress uniform with orders and medals.

The names of *Trafalgar* and *Victory* are often in use as pub titles and in fact examples of both can be found within a few yards of the main gate at Portsmouth Naval Base where visitors may go to see the ship itself. Most such pubs usually have interesting signs illustrating the ship or the battle and some of these are remarkable works of art in their own right. One of the best of these is 'The Trafalgar' at Great Yarmouth where the sign carries a remarkable painting of the battle and included on the sign is the information that the scene depicted shows the situation approximately one hour after Nelson fell and is after the style of an original painting by Clarkson Stanfield. Another inn, 'The Trafalgar Tavern', can be found by visitors to the National Maritime Museum at Greenwich. Sited right on the water's edge just to the east of the Royal Naval College, it was built in 1837 to replace an earlier inn on the same site. Apparently it was frequented by Charles Dickens who placed the wedding breakfast in *Our Mutual Friend* in this setting. It later closed as an inn and was divided up into houses and apartments but, fortunately for the thirsty visitor, it reopened as a tavern in 1965.

In the town centre at Greenwich will be found another variation on the Nelson pub theme — those named after people associated with, or related to, him. In this case it is the 'Admiral Hardy', named after his flag captain at Trafalgar and who later rose to become an admiral. Incidentally, Greenwich also boasts a street called Nelson Road but is by no means unique in this respect — the London A-Z alone lists almost 30 Nelson thoroughfares and the same story can be told in most large cities. In north-east England will be found a cluster of 'Collingwood' pubs and inns named after Nelson's second-in-command at Trafalgar and whose home was in Morpeth, some 10 miles north of Newcastle. Emma Hamilton is also commemorated, although pubs bearing her name are not that common. The most obvious is on the waterfront at Portsmouth, again near the entrance to the Naval Base.

Opposite:
Pub sign to be seen at 'The Victory', Portsmouth, showing the ship under full sail. *ASM*

Above left:
The 'Lady Hamilton' at Portsmouth. Pubs commemorating her name are relatively uncommon.

Above:
'The Trafalgar', Great Yarmouth. A particularly interesting sign showing the battle scene. *ASM*

Other variations relate to pubs bearing the names of ships which took part in Nelson's battles, particularly Trafalgar (the *Téméraire* is one which comes immediately to mind). A little detective work may well uncover a Nelson connection in pub names which, at first glance, would appear to be totally unrelated. A typical example is the 'Hoste Arms', a hotel and inn at Burnham Market in Norfolk. This was originally known as 'The Pitt Arms' but was renamed in 1811 after Admiral Sir William Hoste who had commanded the British fleet which defeated the Austrians at the Battle of Lissa in that year. Sir William was the son of a local clergyman and had first gone to sea as a boy aged 12 under Captain Nelson aboard the frigate *Boreas* and was with him at Tenerife and the Battle of the Nile. Nelson subsequently took a great interest in the boy's career.

Discovering pubs with a Nelson connection can be a fascinating pastime in its own right although definitive listing has yet to be compiled and in this context the author would be pleased to hear of any such pubs, inns or hotels known to readers. In the meantime, if you are passing one, call in and over a quiet drink recall the deeds, struggles, adventures, triumphs, setbacks and all the variety of activities and achievements which made Nelson the great man he was. To the Immortal Memory!

Above:
The 'Admiral Hardy' at Greenwich commemorates Nelson's flag captain at Trafalgar. The sign is based on the portrait in the nearby National Maritime Museum. *ASM*

6: WHERE TO SEE NELSON

Although it is possible to trace the story of Nelson by literally following his footsteps and visiting places, buildings and sites associated with his career, the cost in time and money would be prohibitive for most people. And, although such places provide the context for the events in his life, we can see and learn much more by visiting the museums and other establishments which have spent considerable time and effort in collecting a fascinating assortment of documents, relics, paintings, prints and other memorabilia directly relating to the famous admiral. The following listing gives details of museums and other places at which it is possible to see substantial collections of Nelsonia, much of which has been mentioned or described in this book. Where appropriate, information on opening hours and accessibility is also given and as far as possible these details are correct as of April 1994. However, this information may change and to avoid disappointment it is suggested that it should be checked with the establishment concerned before making a visit. Another point to bear in mind is that most museums are constantly changing and improving their displays and consequently there can be no guarantee that items described in this book will necessarily be on view at any particular time although, in general, museum staffs are always willing to help people with a genuine interest and it is often possible to make arrangements to view items not actually on public display. Finally, although this list covers establishments with a substantial Nelson connection, it is possible to come across one or two items of Nelsonia in museums which otherwise have no particular connection with the subject.

However, before looking at the museums in detail, mention should be made of the remarkable effigy of Nelson currently displayed in the Westminster Abbey museum. This is a very striking creation and perhaps the most lifelike representation to be found today — the three dimensional full-size figure conveying an impression that could never be achieved by a painting (although it should be noted that most experts agree that Nelson was several inches shorter than the 5ft 7in of the wax and wood figure). The pose of the figure is very similar to that in a well-known painting of Nelson by the artist Hoppner, leaning against a rock with one foot drawn back while wearing the full dress uniform of a Vice-Admiral with all his decorations. The wax head and hand were the work of Catherine Andrass, a well-known practitioner of the art of wax modelling at the time, and the final result met with the full approval of Emma Hamilton who herself assisted in the final styling of the hair. This effigy was commissioned by the Abbey museum in 1806 following Nelson's funeral at St Paul's Cathedral, the latter subsequently attracting large numbers of visitors eager to see the tomb in the crypt. As Westminster Abbey relied on the income from visitors to augment its funds, as it does today, a rival attraction was required — hence the effigy of Nelson. Today the effigy is in excellent condition, having been refurbished in 1990-1. It is interesting to note that some items of clothing on the figure actually belonged to Nelson, including the hat, shirt and stockings. The effigy can be viewed in the Abbey museum where it is exhibited alongside similar figures of British Kings and Queens. A small charge is made for admission.

National Maritime Museum

Greenwich, London, SE10 9NF.
Telephone: 0181 858 4422 Fax: 0181 312 6632
Open: 10.00-17.00 Monday to Saturday, 12.00-17.00 Sunday (October to March)
              10.00-18.00 Monday to Saturday, 12.00-18.00 Sunday (April to September)
Charges: Adults £5.50; Concessions £4.50; Children £3.00, Under 5's free; Family ticket
              (2 adults, 3 children) £16.00.

The National Maritime Museum, housed in the magnificent buildings of the former Naval Asylum, must be the starting point for any student of Britain's naval history and houses a fabulous collection of artefacts, paintings, books, plans and photographs. Greenwich itself has naval connections going back as long as Britain has had a Navy as it occupied an important site on the River Thames roughly half-way between the City of London and the Royal Dockyards in the Medway estuary. The well-known Greenwich Naval Hospital was founded in 1694 on the site of a previous Royal Palace where Henry VIII and Elizabeth I were born (coincidentally, both of these famous monarchs did much to foster the growth of British

seapower). The four main blocks of the hospital were constructed between 1696 and 1751 to the plans of the famous architect, Sir Christopher Wren, and were used for this purpose until 1869. From 1873 the site has been occupied by the Royal Naval College which moved here from Portsmouth.

The College stands in the grounds of the oldest of the Royal Parks, established in 1433, which also contains the famous Greenwich Observatory and the Queen's House, built in the 17th century for Anne of Denmark, wife of James I. The house was the earliest example of the classical Palladian style in England although by the beginning of the 19th century it was no longer a royal residence but housed the Naval Asylum, a school for the children of seamen. Massive extension works, in the form of additional wings with connecting colonnades commenced in 1807 and it is these buildings which now house the galleries of the National Maritime Museum. The Asylum, subsequently retitled the Royal Hospital School, moved to Suffolk in 1933 and work then started on converting the buildings for use by the museum which was created by Act of Parliament in 1934. The official opening was carried out by King George VI on 27 April 1937 and the original exhibits included a priceless collection of marine paintings previously displayed in the Painted Hall of the Royal Naval College as well as the contents of the College's Naval Museum. Much of the necessary finance for the museum, including building works and the acquisition of exhibits, was provided by Sir James Caird, a Scottish shipowner and a founder member of the Society for Nautical Research.

Exhibits in the National Maritime Museum are arranged in a number of themed galleries which include subjects such as Discovery and Seapower 1450-1700, Trade and Communications, Exploring the Arctic, and 20th Century Seapower. However, of particular interest is the Nelson gallery situated on the first floor of the west wing. This contains several famous paintings of Nelson and his battles, together with a collection of many items which actually belonged to him, including uniforms, silver, porcelain and furniture. In addition there is a substantial amount of material relating to Emma Hamilton as well as Nelson's colleagues, brother officers and other contemporaries.

Previous page:
Nelson's effigy on display at Westminster Abbey is startlingly realistic. *ASM*

Above:
The National Maritime Museum at Greenwich houses a very large collection of Nelson-related artefacts, as well as covering the general maritime history of Britain. *ASM*

(Note: The National Maritime Museum is planning a series of exhibitions and events over the next 10 years leading up to the bicentennial commemoration of Trafalgar in the year 2005. In connection with this programme, it should be noted that the Nelson Gallery may be closed on occasions in order to allow the displays to be rearranged.)

If time allows, a visit should also be made to the Royal Naval College to view the marvellous Painted Hall where Nelson lay in state prior to his funeral procession up the River Thames in January 1806. As the College is a working establishment, public admission is limited to 14.30-16.30 daily, except Thursdays. Admission is free.

HMS *Victory*

HM Naval Base, Portsmouth, Hants PO1 3LR
Telephone: 01705 819604 (HMS *Victory*). 01705 839766 (Flagship Portsmouth)
Open: March to October: 10.00-17.00 Mon to Sat. 13.00-17.00 Sun.
November to February: 10.00-16.30 Mon to Sat. 1300 -1600 Sun.
Charges: Adults £4.95; Children £2.45; Senior Citizens £4.45. Group rates by arrangement.
(Note: Payment of the admission charge to HMS Victory also entitles the ticket holder to visit the adjacent Royal Naval Museum at no extra charge.)

Nelson's magnificent flagship at the Battle of Trafalgar, HMS *Victory*, is by far the largest and most significant reminder of the man and his achievements. To be able to walk the very decks where Nelson lived, fought and died is a humbling experience and one which is essential to anyone with even a passing interest in his life and times. In many respects, today's generations are fortunate to have access to the ship which for many years lay rotting in Portsmouth harbour and was severely damaged when another ship collided with it in 1902. It was not until the 1920s that a belated effort was made to preserve the ship for posterity and since then repair and restoration work has been continually carried out, although some slight damage was caused by enemy bombing in World War 2. The ship is actually still in commission as a unit of the Royal Navy and serves as the nominal flagship of the C-in-C Portsmouth. Although open to the public, the gundecks and great cabins are still used for ceremonial and official events, while a small permanent crew is aboard to see to the routine and administration of the venerable ship. For many years visitors to the ship were shown around by members of the crew, but recently civilian guides have been recruited although most of these are in fact ex-Navy. Visitors are shown around in groups, for reasons of safety and convenience, visiting the gundecks and the great cabins as well as seeing the actual spot where Nelson died after lying in pain for several hours.

Royal Naval Museum (including the Victory Gallery)

HM Naval Base, Portsmouth, Hants PO1 3LR
Telephone: 01705 733060 Fax: 01705 875806
Open: 10.00-16.30 Daily, November to February
10.00-17.30 Daily, March to October
10.00-18.30 Daily, 1 July to 4 Sept. (Not all galleries necessarily open after 17.30)
Charges: Adults £2.65; Children £1.30 (Permits one further visit in the following 12 month period at no additional charge).

This museum was first opened in 1938 as an adjunct to HMS *Victory* and the original building, immediately opposite the ship, now forms the Victory Gallery which contains an exhibition relevant to the history of the great ship. This traces the career of HMS *Victory* from her launching in 1759, through her illustrious active service which ended in 1812, to her years at anchor followed by restoration and present status. In addition there are many items associated with the men who served aboard her including medals and personal

Above:
The Victory Gallery is situated alongside the ship and forms part of the Royal Naval Museum at Portsmouth. *ASM*

Left:
The main part of the Royal Naval Museum is housed in these imposing colonnaded buildings, originally used as storehouses during the Napoleonic Wars. *ASM*

possessions while on the upper floor various models show the development of the wooden fighting ship up to the middle of the 19th century. Also housed here is the actual barge which carried Nelson's body on its melancholy journey up the Thames from Greenwich to the Admiralty steps on the occasion of his state funeral in 1806.

The rest of the Royal Naval Museum has been developed over the past 30 years and occupies a series of former storehouses built in Nelson's time to service his great fleet. One of these houses the Lambert McCarthy Gallery where an extensive collection of Nelsonia is on view. This great collection was built up by an American lady, Mrs Lily Lambert McCarthy CBE, the wife of Mr John G. McCarthy of Greenwich, Connecticut. Her interest in the Royal Navy in general, and Nelson in particular, was sparked off by contacts with British sailors from HMS *Asbury*, a shore establishment set up in America during World War 2. Her collection subsequently became one of the most important of its kind and in 1971 she generously donated it to the Royal Naval Museum. Appropriately, it was embarked (with great care) aboard the Type 12 frigate HMS *Lowestoft* at Washington Navy Yard in October 1971. Nelson, of course, served aboard an earlier HMS *Lowestoft* in the West Indies during 1777/78. After passage to England, the collection was installed in its present location and officially opened to the public by Mrs Lambert McCarthy on 4 May 1972.

Royal Marine Museum

Eastney, Portsmouth
Telephone: 01705 819385
Open: 09.30-17.00 Daily, May to September
10.00-1630 Daily, October to April
Charges: Adults £3.00; Children £1.50; Senior Citizens £2.00. Family and Group rates also available.

Housed in the impressive former Officers' Mess of the Royal Marine barracks overlooking the Solent at the extreme eastern end of Portsmouth's and Southsea's seafront, this museum is primarily concerned with showing the history of the Royal Marines from their inception as the Duke of York and Albany's Maritime Regiment of Foot in 1664 to their present role as the spearhead of the Navy's amphibious forces. By Nelson's time the Marines were an established and vital part of a warship's complement and a section of the museum is devoted to the bravery and heroism of marines who served with Nelson and took part in his battles. There are letters, medals and personal possessions, and particular reference is made to the Battle of Trafalgar where two officers made sketches and watercolours at the time to provide rare contemporary illustrations of the battle. There is also a letter, written by Nelson and dated May 1804, laying down the duties of the Royal Marine gunners serving aboard the bomb ketches of the Channel Fleet.

The Maritime Museum, Bucklers Hard

Beaulieu, Hampshire SO42 7XB
Telephone: 01590 616203
Open: Daily 10.00-18.00 Easter to Spring Bank Holiday
Daily 10.00-21.00 Spring Bank Holiday to September
Daily 10.00-16.30 Winter Months (Closed Christmas Day)
Charges: Adults £2.60; Children £1.75, Senior Citizens £2.10

This museum is beautifully situated beside the upper reaches of the Beaulieu River and incorporates what was once a busy shipyard where wooden men-of-war were built for the Royal Navy. Of particular significance is the fact that HMS *Agamemnon*, a 64-gun Third Rate, was built here and launched in 1781. She was the first line-of-battle ship which Nelson commanded, taking up his appointment in 1793 after having spent five years ashore on half pay. Still visible today is the site of the slipway where she was built, while the museum has a fascinating collection of detailed models showing the *Agamemnon* and other ships built at the yard. There are also several personal items related to Nelson on display, including a

complete set of his baby clothes — a must for any student of Nelson's life. The museum also features an extensive and detailed diorama showing how the yard would have looked a few days before the launch of HMS *Agamemnon* and giving an insight into how ships were built at that time. Outside the museum gallery, the original terraces of cottages which housed the shipyard workers are still in use and line the approach to the site of the former slipways. Some of these have been incorporated into the museum and show how people lived and worked during the shipyard's heyday in the latter half of the 18th century. The museum itself was originally based on the New Inn at the top end of one of the terraces and was opened by Lord Mountbatten in 1963 although it has been considerably extended since then. At the lower end of the other terrace is the 'Master Builder's Hotel' which offers bar and café facilities, as well as accommodation if required. One of the hotel rooms, overlooking the river, is preserved as the office of the Master Shipwright, Henry Adams, who was responsible for the building of many ships including Nelson's *Agamemnon*.

Above:
Entrance to the Bucklers Hard Maritime Museum on the shores of the Beaulieu River. *ASM*

The Maritime Museum for East Anglia

Marine Parade, Great Yarmouth, Norfolk NR30 2EN
Telephone: 01493 842267
Open: 10.00-17.00, Sunday to Friday from the first Sunday after the Spring Bank Holiday to the end of September. Also for two weeks at Easter.
Charge: Adults £1.00; Children £0.50; Concessions £0.60. (Ticket allows admission to other Yarmouth museums).

Great Yarmouth has a number of associations with Nelson and, of course, he was born in Norfolk. The Maritime Museum is situated on the town's main seafront but is overshadowed by the many amusement halls and fairgrounds which line the Marine Parade. Most of the museum's displays relate to the maritime history of this part of the coast with emphasis being made on such activities as fishing and the modern offshore industry. Nelson exhibits are restricted to a portion of the drape from his funeral car and a recently commissioned accurate replica of his full dress uniform as displayed in the National Maritime Museum at Greenwich, together with a selection of prints and engravings. However, the museum does possess an excellent library which can be made available, by arrangement, for research purposes. On the shelves are such treasures as a complete run of the Naval Chronicle, Mahan's biography of Nelson, a bound volume of Nelson's letters and dispatches as collected and arranged by Sir H. Nicolas. Also present are two complete sets of Dr Campbell's *Lives of the Admirals* which are a source of much detail on Nelson and his famous contemporaries.

The Nelson Museum

Priory St, Monmouth, Gwent NP5 3XA
Telephone: 01600 713519
Open: 10.00-13.00, 14.00-17.00, Monday to Saturday (inc Bank Holidays)
14.00-17.00 Sunday
Charges: Adults £1.00; Children free when accompanied by an adult. Group rates by arrangement. (Ticket allows admission to other establishments including Caldicot Castle.)

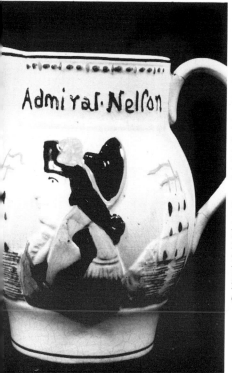

The Nelson Collection belonging to Lady Llangattock of Hendre, near Monmouth, was bequeathed to the town in 1924 and for many years was displayed in a museum housed in a former gymnasium in Glendower Street. In 1969 the collection was moved to its present location in the New Market Hall rebuilt behind its original facade after being destroyed by fire in 1963. Lady Llangattock was an avid collector of Nelson memorabilia but also has a claim to fame as the mother of C. S. Rolls, one of the founder partners of the famous Rolls-Royce company. Charles Rolls learnt to fly in 1910 and was awarded Pilot Certificate No 2 by the Royal Aero Club. Later that year he was the first man to make a two way crossing of the English Channel by air but he was tragically killed in a flying accident during a display at Bournemouth in

Opposite:
The Maritime Museum for East Anglia at Great Yarmouth, a town with many Nelson connections. *ASM*

Left:
A colourful commemorative Liverpool-ware jug. *Nelson Museum, Monmouth*

July 1910. A memorial to him stands in the main square of Monmouth.

The museum itself houses a fascinating collection and the main gallery is laid out to illustrate the life of Nelson by means of prints, paintings, letters, and personal items, all presented with informative captions. Also on display is the substantial Llangattock collection which includes many of Nelson's personal possessions. The museum also has a substantial library of books relating to Nelson and his times as well as important collections of his letters and other manuscripts. These latter consist of papers which originally belonged to Lady Nelson and others which were originally in the possession of Emma Hamilton. These, with other documents, form an important, and not yet fully researched, source of detailed information on Nelson and his life.

Admiral Ld Nelson mortally wounded by a Musket Ball in the ever memorable Victory at Trafalgar on 21 Oct. 19 Sail of the Enemy struck their Colours 1 blew up in the Action B. run away 4 of them were afterward captured by Sir Richard Strachan off Ferrol 4 Nov. 1805.

Left:
A charming study of Nelson's daughter as a young woman. This miniature, executed on ivory, is in the possession of the Nelson Museum. *Nelson Museum, Monmouth*

Above:
This painting on glass is one of many representations of the death of Nelson. *Nelson Museum, Monmouth*

Chatham Historic Dockyard

Chatham, Kent ME4 4TE
Telephone: 01634 812551
Open: 10.00-18.00, Wednesday to Sunday (and Bank Holidays), April to October
10.00-16.30, Wednesday, Saturday, Sunday, November to March.
Charge: Adults £5.60; Children £3.60. Half price admission on second visit within
12 months. (Family ticket: 2 adults and 4 children, £15.00.)

The main interest here is in the building and repair of the ships of Nelson's Navy. The drydock where HMS *Victory* was built can still be seen and there is the very interesting Wooden Walls feature, an animated display housed in buildings dating from the 18th century which shows how a man-of-war was ordered, laid down, built, launched and commissioned. Around the old dockyard are many buildings which would have been known to Nelson and there is also a display of ordnance of the period where the development of naval cannon and gun carriages can be traced.

Other Sites

The list shown on the previous pages is by no means exhaustive but does cover those places where there is a significant Nelson interest. Many other establishments sometimes contain small collections and among these one of the most prominent is the popular Castle Museum in the centre of Norwich which has a small Nelson display, the contents of which are described in Chapter 3. Also in Norfolk, the town museum at King's Lynn has one or two items of interest. Many other municipal museums will have the odd Nelson item, particularly commemorative ware and examples of the many medals struck in honour of Nelson and his victories, while examination of the contents of many stately homes will often throw up something of interest.

Left:
Virtually every portrait of Nelson shows him dressed in naval uniform. This watercolour and ink sketch by an unknown artist shows him in civilian dress. *Nelson Museum, Monmouth*